27	Sea sickness
49	Sail Plan + jib furling novelty .
50	Brooks + Gatehouse Hornet Unit .
50	Life Raft + dinghies
51	B+G Horatio unit
51	Radio
55	Balaclava
62	Insurance
68	Thermal underwear
68	Rigging
88	Nav-Lights
119	Keelbolt leaks
122	Oil Skins
122 + 177.	Roller furling
126	Sestral Porthole Compass
131	Harrods for tinned goods !
145	Tomatoes !
159	Radar detector
178 + 179	Halyards

Blue Water Green Skipper

Stuart Woods

STANFORD MARITIME : LONDON

STANFORD MARITIME LIMITED

(Member Company of the George Philip Group)

12 Long Acre, London, WC2E 9LP

First published in Great Britain 1977
Copyright © Stuart Woods 1977

Filmset and printed in Great Britain by
BAS Printers Limited, Wallop, Hampshire

ISBN 0 540 07168 4

Acknowledgements

I believe I have mentioned nearly everyone who helped my project in the text of this book, but inevitably I may have left someone out in the rush to publication. If I have done so, I hope the persons left out will believe that they are not forgotten. It was a solo event, but literally dozens of people played absolutely essential parts in the preparations.

I am particularly indebted to Angela Green of the Promotions Department of *The Observer* for her assistance in helping me learn what happened to other competitors, and for the loan of her logbook and records.

I owe special thanks to my editor, Peter Coles of Stanford Maritime, for his continuing interest in my project and his hard work on this book, and to his colleagues Rosemary Lister and Mike Davies for their help.

George and Elizabeth Golemis, of the Newport Loft, were very kind to me and made sure that *Golden Harp* was cared for and sailed after I left Newport, seeing that she survived a hurricane undamaged.

Finally, I feel I must thank Ron Holland again for his genius, his expertise, his hard work and his friendship. I commend him to you as the designer of your next yacht.

This book is for
Mike and Lizzie McMullen

Contents

Contents

The cover illustrations and photograph on page 80 were taken by Ron Holland.

The Race chart reproduced on page 137 is by kind permission of *The Observer* and the photographs on pages 145, 146 and 189 (right) are by Chris Smith of *The Observer*.

Illustrations on pages 155 and 138 are courtesy of *Cruising World* and the top photograph on page 143 is by Helen Simpson and the lower by Johnathan Eastland.

Photograph on page 156 by Alistair Black and the top left illustration on page 189 by Rob Humphries.

Book One
1 Some sort of beginning

I stood in this place for the second time in forty minutes, a small, neat bay, surrounded by low hills, white cottages, a ruined mansion and an unspecified number of dairy cattle, chewing their way through the morning. This choppy stretch of water was covered by a churning grey sky and contained half a dozen small, plastic buoys and an old stone pier. Perhaps 'stood' constitutes sloppy use of the language, for about forty knots of wind had me leaning at an unnatural angle to the perpendicular and the hairs on the leeward side of my body standing at an equally unnatural angle to my skin. I had not yet learned that a mild, sunny beginning to an Irish morning does not obviate the necessity for a sheepskin coat and gumboots at a slightly later hour, and I could not, for the life of me, see the Galway Bay Sailing Club.

I drove back to the Thatched Pub in Oranmore and explained my problem to its keeper. As he had already done twice on that morning, he began patiently to direct me to Rinville Bay. I interrupted to explain that I was certain I had found the bay, but could not find the clubhouse.

'Ah,' said George the innkeeper, with the raised eyebrows of the enlightened, 'there's not a club*house*, y'see; there's just the *club*, like.'

I gaped at him uncomprehendingly, unable to shake my preconception of the neat building, the flagpole and the ruddy-faced chaps gathered in the net-draped bar. George leapt into the silence, which every Irishman abhors: 'There's just the club, and I'd say they're not likely to be out just yet.' It was March, I had to give him that, but it was a Sunday too, and the paperback I had read had led me to believe that your enthusiastic yachtsman, if not actually on the water nowabouts, would at least be varnishing or splicing something in preparation for the event, and if not that, knocking a few back and talking about it at the very least.

George fixed his gaze on the Guinness pump handle before him, trying hard to be helpful. 'Pierce Purcell,' he said, looking relieved. 'You'd want to speak to Pierce Purcell, he's the secretary or one of the people, like, and you'd find him in the book.'

The Irish Department of Posts and Telegraphs, because of the small size of the country, the low density of the population and its own extreme reluctance to provide any of them with a telephone, has managed to gather all the nation's telephone listings into just one directory, which is, in size, roughly equal to the combined bulk of *The Old Testament, The New Testament,* the *I Ching* and *The Joy of Sex.* It proved to contain at least a page of closely-spaced Purcells, far too many of them P.'s, P.J.'s and even Pierces, and none of them in Galway. George tried again.

'Ferdia O'Riordan,' he said, this time with real conviction. The book offered us even more O'Riordans than Purcells, but no Ferdias in Galway. 'The Bank of Ireland,' said George with finality. 'That's where he works, at the branch in Salthill.' But in Ireland only the pubs are open on a Sunday, so I thanked George and postponed my search for sailing yet another day.

Sailing had been wafting around the hindmost part of my head since the summer of 1966, when friends had invited me to their summer home in Castine, Maine, and back in my native USA, taken me sailing every day the wind blew. I had been enchanted with the notion that one could move across the face of the waters, fuelled by nothing more than the wind, and I had resolved that if ever I were domiciled in any reasonable proximity to the sea I would learn to sail upon it. I thought, even, that since so much of the world was covered with water and since it lapped against so many interesting places, that I should like to sail right the way round, stopping everywhere.

Eventually, I finished a ten-year hitch in New York advertising, did another three in London and then, propelled by a life-long desire to write A Novel, hied myself to the west of Ireland, to County Galway, to Lough Cutra Castle, near Gort, where I resided not in the castle, but in the adjacent stableyard, in a flat. I spent two days a week in Dublin, writing television commercials and ads for an advertising agency, and the rest of the time in County Galway, writing my novel or, at least, thinking about it.

Lough Cutra was an ideal place—four hundred acres of grounds, twelve hundred acres of lake and enough peace and quiet to make it very difficult to find an excuse not to write. To live this sort of existence you have either to be very lucky or very single. Looking back, I still find it difficult to believe I was able to get away with this for two years.

Soon after my arrival in Ireland, in early 1973, I perceived that it was surrounded by water, and the sailing notion, so long displaced by an absorbing career and an athletic social life in New York and London, began to winnow its way into my frontal lobe. I bought a book which suggested that the way to go about learning to sail was to start with a small dinghy, then work up to larger things as desired and funds dictated. For several winter weeks I scoured the west, looking for a small boat to buy or someone who knew where to buy one or someone who knew someone who knew. Just when I was beginning to think that I was the only person in the counties Galway, Clare and Mayo who realized that Ireland was an island, a friend in Galway, who believed that water should be fished in and not sailed upon, admitted that he had heard of the existence of a sailing club in or near Galway City.

He was pretty cagey about it all, but still, I had managed to penetrate the alleged club's apparent security arrangements to the point where I now had an actual name and an actual telephone number to call. Journeying to the public telephone in Mrs Piggot's Grocery Store in Gort, I gave the operator the number, inserted the required coinage into the instrument and waited the customary seven minutes to be connected. To my surprise, there really was a Ferdia O'Riordan at the Bank of Ireland in Salthill, and he very generously invited me to join him for a sail the following Sunday, behaving as if the Galway Bay Sailing Club were common knowledge and had nothing whatever to hide.

During the week which followed I reread my book on sailing and bought another, wishing to be as *au fait* as possible without actually having set foot in any sort of boat for seven years. The Sunday arrived and I again found myself at Rinville. Nothing had changed, except that the wind was blowing slightly less hard and the temperature had crept up a degree or two. The place was still deserted, and I sat in my battered Mini, chatting idly with Fred, a 4-pound, five-week-old example of the Golden Labrador breed, who graciously permitted me to share my flat with him. At last, a car materialized next to mine, towing a boat covered with canvas. From this car emerged Ferdia O'Riordan, his very pretty wife, and two irresistible little girls, with whom Fred evidenced an immediate empathy. Leaving the two children and the puppy rolling in the grass, we removed the canvas from the boat, revealing a gleaming example of the GP Fourteen class, erected the mast, bent on the sails and trundled the lot at breakneck speed down the rocky shore. Ferdia and I stripped off our shoes and socks, rolled up our trouser legs and waded into the icy water. In a trice, I was experiencing again that giddy sensation of motion over water which had so mesmerized me in Maine seven summers before.

We thrashed about Rinville Bay, Ferdia issuing a steady stream of calm instructions, I trying to remember what I had read during the last week, while shifting my weight about in such a way as to keep us upright, and endeavouring to cope with sheets, cleats and centreboard. 'We're nearly planing now,' Ferdia said at one point. I made a mental note to find out what 'planing' meant. It had a familiar ring.

Back on shore, while gathering my wits about me again, Ferdia, who turned out to be the Club Secretary, produced a membership form and relieved me of a cheque. We discussed what sort of boat I should buy and the consensus seemed to be a Mirror, a ten-foot ten-inch plywood dinghy whose design had been sponsored by the newspaper of the same name, which could be bought ready-built or in kit form, and which was the most popular boat in the club.

Considering that in an entire year of wood-working classes in high school I had produced only one wobbly bookcase and half a lamp base, I thought the ready-built form of the boat appealed most, although I was assured that twelve girl scouts had once built one in eight hours. (Twelve girl scouts represent a multiplication of my woodworking talents by a factor of twenty-four.) Since demand for these little boats was high and supply slow, I would probably have to wait a bit for delivery, but the Club, it was disclosed, owned two Mirrors for the use of members who did not themselves own boats, so I would be able to sail in the meantime. Also, the Club was holding a boat show in a couple of weeks' time, and there I would be able to peruse a number of other craft before purchasing.

During the time remaining until the boat show I dropped by Rinville several times more, and on one occasion was invited out for a sail in a twenty-foot dayboat by a rumpled fellow of about my own age, who looked as I imagined a Galway fisherman looked and, to my American ear, sounded. It is a measure of my discernment in these matters at that stage of my Irish experience that he turned out to be the Minister for Local Government.

The First Annual Galway Boat Show took place in the car park of the Salthill Hotel. On display were a dozen assorted dinghies and powerboats, some fishing and diving gear and other water-oriented paraphernalia. Also on display was a gleaming new Mirror dinghy which was being raffled as a fund-raising project for the club, and which I did not win. However, a large Dutchman and I unearthed one of the Club Mirrors from Ferdia O'Riordan's garage and, after an hour or so of puzzling over fittings, rigging and sails, got it afloat.

We pottered about between Black Rock Pier and the Margaretta Buoy in the middle of Galway Bay, tacking and gybing the little boat in a lovely breeze. My reading programme was paying off handsomely, things making a great deal more sense than on my first outing with Ferdia. I had another short sail with another member, and then dropped him off at the pier.

My recent reading had included Sir Francis Chichester's book, *Gypsy Moth Circles the World* and Joshua Slocum's superb account of his three-year circumnavigation in the last century, the first by a man alone. No doubt these had served as some sort of inspiration, for I pushed off in the little dinghy and sailed her singlehanded out to the buoy and back, ajangle at the newness of it all and terrified of capsizing the thing in sight of the crowd on the pier. This was a kind of high several notches above sailing with somebody else. Now, for better or for drowning, I had the thing all to myself, my first command, as it were, and I relished the experience. Tacking around the buoy went much as the book had said it should; the dinghy scooted across the water, seemingly in defiance of, rather than in harmony with, the laws of nature, and I returned to shore lightheaded, as if having breathed an enriched atmosphere.

I felt it was some sort of beginning, though of what I wasn't certain, and to my distant fantasy of sailing around the world was added the even more fantastic notion of doing some part of it alone, and although the next time I sailed a boat alone the circumstances were much more exotic and the possible consequences far more serious, the special euphoria of that first, short, singlehanded voyage remained unrivaled.

2 Learning a bit

Carol, Fred and I arrived at Rosturk Castle on a Friday evening in June, the Club dinghy in tow behind the Mini. Carol, an old friend from both New York and London days, was passing through Ireland on her way back to live in the States, and we had been invited up to County Mayo for the Westport Show. The dinghy, much used and a bit battered, was for sailing in Westport Bay, for Rosturk Castle is situated on one of the most beautiful inlets of that very beautiful body of water.

Sunday we went sailing, which was not as simple as it sounds. The inlet on which Rosturk stands habitually dries out twice a day, when the tide recedes, leaving a quarter-mile or so of lovely golden sand to replace the water, which ends up some distance from the castle. Since our time of rising and breakfasting coincided with low water, it was necessary for someone to come with us down the long strip of sand to the water's edge in the Mini and, after the dinghy had been launched, return to the house with the car and Fred, who, in the two or three times I had sailed since my debut, had shown himself to be not much in the way of a yachtsman. He either fell asleep with his head on the tiller or strolled about the decks until he fell into the water. He was, at least, good for man overboard drills.

We successfully launched the dinghy and sailed off into an already increasing breeze. Westport Bay is filled with islands, reputedly 365 of them, and it had been our intention to sail among them for a sufficient number of hours for the tide to allow us to sail right up to the doorstep of the castle. However, on the water everything looks a bit different; the wind blows a bit harder, the waves are a bit steeper and, on top of everything else, it was starting to drizzle. I am not sure if I had confided the state of my experience to Carol, but she seemed willing to sail wherever I wished, so I probably hadn't.

We beat out from behind an island and the wind and waves both grew in strength—not to an alarming state, but sailing the boat required great concentration. There was little time for absorbing the beauties of Westport Bay. Carol, incredibly, managed to light a cigarette. We agreed that a shorter sail than originally conceived was in order. We sailed around the island and headed into the channel separating it from the shore where the castle stood. Then we were running, that is, the wind was directly behind us, and so were the waves. We began to surf in a small way, which was exciting, and then we 'broached to', which was a little too exciting. When a boat which is running broaches, it appears suddenly to change its mind about the direction in which it is sailing and to attempt to change its course, swinging abruptly around and abeam to the wind. This action, in proper concert with a passing wave, can cause the occupants of a dinghy to become swimmers. We were wearing buoyancy aids, but these did not make the prospect seem any more inviting. We broached twice before I learned to anticipate the movement and keep us on a straight course.

We drove on up the inlet until the boat touched the sand, then we hopped out. We were still a quarter-mile from the castle. I sent Carol up for the car and trailer while I got the sails down and stood in the water, holding the dinghy. The tide was coming in quite fast, now.

Carol arrived with the car and backed the trailer down to the edge of the water, which was still several yards away from the Mini. I unhitched the trailer, pushed it down to the dinghy and asked Carol to help me lift the boat onto it. This seemed to take no more than a minute or two. I turned to start pulling the trailer toward the car and saw, to my horror, that water was lapping at the hubcaps of the Mini. The tide was moving faster than I had realized.

I dropped the trailer, dived into the car and started the engine. I breathed a sigh of relief. I put it into gear and tried to drive out of the water. The wheels promptly buried themselves in the sand. The front axles were now resting on the bottom. I sent Carol back to the house for help, while I tried vainly to rock the car out of the sand by shifting alternately into first gear and reverse. The wheels spun happily back and forth, but remained in precisely the same position. I got out of the car and looked around for help. Far up the inlet, perhaps half-a-mile away, I saw a man driving a tractor, towing a trailer-load of seaweed across the sand. I jumped up and down and waved. He seemed not to see me. I blew the horn of the car repeatedly, but clearly the sound would never penetrate the noise of the tractor engine. There was no one else in sight.

I got back into the car and raced the engine; it seemed terribly important, somehow, to keep it going. Then I began to blow a signal on the horn—dot dot dot, dash dash dash, dot dot dot—SOS, the only Morse code I had ever been able to learn. The water continued to rise, and I continued to honk my signal. I could see Carol; she was not quite halfway to the castle, tired already from her first hike back for the car. The water was now beginning to creep over the door sills. I considered abandoning ship, but continued to honk. Far up the beach a figure was running toward the tractor, pointing my way. The tractor changed direction. Now it was a question of which would arrive first, the tractor or the tide. The tide seemed to be winning. The carpets were now under water.

The tractor moved faster than I could have believed possible and arrived accompanied by a German guest at the castle, who had been awakened from his nap by the sound of my Morse SOS. Thank God the German boy scouts did a better job of teaching its members Morse Code than, in my experience, the American branch. Just at the point where I was about to be sailing a Mini instead of a Mirror, the car came free of the sand. It even ran for a couple of miles before dying. The salt water had eaten away the fuel pump and one or two other essentials. If anybody knows of a more graphic way for a budding dinghy sailor to be taught about the tides I don't want to hear about it.

The next thing I learned about sailing was that some boats, for no readily apparent reason, go faster than others. I learned this in the most embarrassing possible way for an adult, from children.

While I waited for my new Mirror to be built and delivered, a period of ten weeks, I tried racing the Club Mirror in the regular Sunday and Wednesday afternoon events. In the beginning I had had no interest whatever in racing, but I soon found that cruising in a dinghy was not especially appealing, particularly if the wind died and the bloody thing had to be paddled home. So, having memorized about three of the several dozen International Yacht Racing Union Rules, I grabbed a passing teenager for a crew and thrashed my way around the buoys, losing to everybody except two tiny individuals who had capsized and retired. Fortunately, I had a number of excuses with which to console myself: the Club boat leaked like a sieve; the sails were old and worn; the bottom was rough with age, and so forth. I bought a dinghy pump, and this kept my feet drier, but my ego remained damp. My new boat would solve all this, I was sure.

The new boat helped. I collected it, all dark blue and shiny, and named it *Fred*, in the hope that it would like the water as much as the puppy. It liked the water, and I finished third in my first race, but that was as high as I could scramble for several weeks. I began to investigate all the go-fast fittings and ideas allowed by the measurement rules of the

Racing *Fred* in Galway Bay.

Mirror Class Association. I grew accustomed to being handed small, brown paper bags in yacht chandleries, while a supercilious clerk intoned, 'That will be £30, please.' I began reading the specialist books on racing and poring over the yachting magazines, looking for that elusive instruction which would send me surging to the fore of the fleet. And lo, I began to improve. I began to beat the smaller children. Progress.

A big problem, of course, was that I did not have a regular crew. Most grown men who race in the smaller dinghy classes breed sons and daughters for this purpose, lashing them to the boat as soon as they are old enough to be shouted at. In my bachelor state I was so far behind in this game that it would have taken six or seven years to catch up. So I had to be content to borrow the odd kid when Dad was away or too hungover to make the start. Adults were too heavy, learned too slowly and had too low a humiliation threshold for crewing a Mirror dinghy. Once, at a two-day meet on Lough Derg, I persuaded a grown-up acquaintance new to sailing to crew for me. In the first race we did miserably, our combined weight destroying us in very light winds. In the second race, after a lunch at which we consoled ourselves with a litre of plonk, a huge wind appeared from nowhere, capsized us and left us riding to anchor in the half-filled dinghy, drinking still more plonk and waiting for the crash boat to come and take us away. His wife phoned the next day and said he wasn't well and couldn't make races three and four.

So for the rest of the season I found crews wherever I could and continued to chase, and occasionally even beat, the leaders, all of whom were in their mid-teens except my arch-rival Dr Tom Coll, an alleged adult with an enthusiastic younger brother for a crew. We exchanged good natured abuse ashore and afloat, and whenever I beat him he would pretend to sulk for a week.

The highlight of the season was the National Championships, a week-long event held at Lough Derg. I arrived crewless, as usual, but found a twelve-year-old Dublin girl named Caroline, who was small for her age. She turned out to be a shrewd and experienced dinghy sailor and her small weight helped make up for mine. We finished thirty-ninth out of a fleet of sixty. With luck we could have done better, but still, I had never before beaten twenty-one boats.

It ended the season if not on a high note, at least on one which would hum through my mind all through the following winter.

3 Hooked

I was thirty-five years old when I first sailed that Mirror dinghy—in my late youth, one might say. My figure had assumed those slightly more generous proportions so attractive in a person of my age, and just a tiny bit more of my scalp was exposed to the sunshine than had been true a few years before. (Someone once described me, unkindly, as 'balding'. This is not strictly true. I am balding only if you are taller than I am and stand behind me.) This is a time of life when a man has a duty to his family, his society and probably the United Nations to go forth and painfully extract seventy-five or a hundred thousand dollars a year from his nation's gross national product and then plough back about twenty-five per cent more than that into mortgage payments, insurance premiums, school fees for his children, analysts' fees for his wife, and quadraphonic sound and electrocardiograms for himself. It is a known fact that unless everybody does this there will be another depression and a Communist Takeover, followed shortly by a Nuclear Holocaust. I know that it was terribly irresponsible of me, but at this critical juncture of my life my existence was ruled by the compulsion to find a way to make a ten-foot ten-inch plywood dinghy go faster than that of the thirteen-year-old kid down the street. I know this is no way for a grown man to behave, but I couldn't help it. I was hooked.

This confusing condition becomes even more inexplicable if one examines my career in sport up to that time, which, believe me, will not take long. In my school days in Manchester, Georgia, I fought a pitched battle for two years with a co-student to see who could become the worst football player in the history of Manchester High School. He never had a chance. Every winter for four years I went out for the basketball team and was cut from the squad after the first two weeks of practice, which the coach considered a decent interval, given the state of my native ability. I did, however, make the tennis team in my senior year—mostly, I believe, because I owned a tennis racket and only three other boys went out for the team. I was instrumental in the loss of every doubles match we played that year, and for my efforts was awarded a school letter in track. The coach said something about having ordered too many track letters and not enough tennis. When I lived in London I played tennis about twice a week in Battersea Park, where I could acquit myself fairly well in mixed doubles if the girls were bad enough.

And now, in the middle of my life and with that record behind me, I found myself consumed by and even achieving a kind of competitive mediocrity in a new sport. And when the season ended things got worse. I pored over every yachting publication available, taking notes. I trudged up and down the aisles of chandleries examining the available equipment minutely, buying everything which held the promise of that extra tenth of a knot of speed. I read ever more advanced books on technique—books about roll tacking, spinnaker handling, eliminating weather helm. I ordered a new mast from Collar's of Oxford and new sails from Jack Holt. I memorized the yacht racing rules. When spring came I started screwing and bolting the fruits of my winter's search to the dinghy.

And then a wonderful thing happened. Harry McMahon bought an Enterprise. An Enterprise is a larger, heavier boat than a Mirror, and Harry needed a larger, heavier crew to help keep it upright. This size requirement shanghied Harry's bemused wife into action and his eldest son, Dairmuid, out of it. Dairmuid had all of the qualities I could have wanted in a son of my own. He was eleven years old, skinny enough to help make up for my bulk and had been shouted at by his father for two seasons in a Mirror. He knew more than enough to keep me out of trouble and he wasn't big enough to yell at me when I made a stupid mistake. The day Harry showed up with the Enterprise I offered to adopt Dairmuid. Harry compromised by offering to lend him to me for the summer in return for a good price on my old Mirror sails. Everybody was happy except, possibly, Dairmuid. Nobody asked him.

At last I had a regular crew of my own. At last the boat was light enough to sail in light winds. At last the spinnaker was being used well. At last I was being beaten by adults instead of children, and a lot of the time I was beating the adults. Life was full of meaning.

Dairmuid and I campaigned the boat hard that summer, going to as many open and regional meetings as we could manage. We sailed fast, but too often made one gigantic, unforgiveable mistake in a race—enough to put us fourth or fifth instead of first. Still, it was hugely satisfying and a wonderful excuse for not writing, something every writer desperately needs.

We looked forward eagerly to the Mirror National Championships, when boats from all over Ireland (and some from England) would congregate at Sligo for a week of battling around the buoys. Championship week arrived, and so did Dairmuid's appendix. Dairmuid was desolated. I was suicidal. Harry offered to take his son's place.

A fully rigged Mirror weighs 150 pounds, which means that Harry and I weighed a lot more than twice as much as the boat. This disadvantage, combined with the fact that Harry and I were both used to skippering and not crewing, giving orders and not taking them, made things a bit tense. In the first race I completely screwed up the rather complicated gate start, to the extent that we started the race about a hundred yards behind the last of the other seventy boats. This seemed to annoy Harry. Then the wind went very light, and, since we weighed so much, we had little chance of catching up. We retired from this race, because, as I explained to Harry, I would rather have an 'R' on the scoreboard next to my name than a '71st'. Harry had a number of brief, but incisive comments to make about this and other of my decisions during the race. The second race went a lot better. I screwed up the start again, but there was more wind and we managed to work our way up to about twenty-fifth. Our relationship as skipper and crew was improving, too. Harry only threatened to get out and walk once.

Then came the third race and, with it, the wind. The wind blew and the waves got bigger—ideal conditions for Harry and me with our weight, and bad for the small kids. Wonderful. We started well, but then sailed off on a tack by ourselves. Still, we seemed to be doing fairly well, concentrating hard on keeping the boat as upright as possible and sailing fast. As we rounded a mark and relative positions became a bit better defined I looked around to see how we were doing. 'Harry,' I said, 'I know this seems odd, but an awful lot of those boats seem to be *behind* us.' Harry shot me a look of withering disbelief and looked around. His face unfolded like a rose.

'Jesus,' he said, 'I think you're right.' We finished eighth out of seventy boats, better than either of us had ever done at a National, and we were now in a position where, if we finished well in the fourth and last race, we might place in the top ten overall, a circumstance beyond our most lurid fantasies. But the wind continued to rise, and finally, because there were so many small kids involved, the last race was cancelled. But there was still glory. We were given a prize for being the oldest and heaviest crew and we had finished twenty-ninth out of seventy boats. It was my finest hour.

4 Hooked anew

There had been talk of Fireballs for some weeks now. A Fireball is a high performance racing dinghy with a big sail plan and a trapeze for the crew. It was a different kettle of fish from a Mirror, but four of us were pretty hot on the idea. I assembled costs on everything from the hiring of a mould (we were going to build them ourselves) to spars and sails, but, one by one, people dropped out, and anyway something else happened that pointed me in a new direction. Dave Fitzgerald asked me to go sailing with him.

Dave owned a Snapdragon 24, a tubby little cruising yacht of some age, but of considerable charm, at least to me. He had sailed her to France earlier in the summer and was bringing her back in stages. The final stage was from Valentia, an island just off southwest Ireland, to Galway, and he invited me to join him and his regular crew in bringing her up. I suspected that he had run out of people to ask who actually knew what they were doing aboard a cruising boat and had been reduced to accepting a dinghy sailor, but I leapt at the chance, having never actually *been* anywhere on a sailboat. I had spent two summers sailing triangular courses, and the idea of floating from one place to another was enormously appealing. This was much closer to sailing around the world.

We drove down to Valentia on a Friday evening, the plan being to set out from Knightstown, on the island, early the next morning and sail to Kilronan, in the Aran Islands, and thence on the Sunday into Galway. It was a long drive to Valentia, but we moved quickly, it being important to get to Knightstown before the pubs closed. We slept quite comfortably on the boat (*Pegeen* she was called), and we got up early enough for the morning BBC marine weather forecast. Five minutes later we were asleep again, as the BBC was forecasting a possible gale

Force eight, which seemed to be more wind than Dave wanted to face with a hangover. We passed a sunny day idly, and the gale never materialized. Next morning, after another night at the pub, we overslept and got away later than planned. We had to beat out through the Blasket Sound in a short, choppy sea and, having been anxious about the possibility of being seasick on my first coastal passage, I had taken a sea sickness pill, which rendered me semi-conscious for the first couple of hours. I recovered by midmorning and found us broad reaching up the coast with a nice Force four southwesterly breeze behind us.

The company was good. Dave was a large man with a meaty nose who has been known to sign autographs for Tommy Cooper, and when he is not sailing he runs the Tynagh Mines in County Galway. Philip, his other crew, is smaller than Dave and his nose is less meaty, but he is working on that. They are both very Irish, which is to say they never drink between eight and ten a.m. and never stop talking. There was a constant stream of banter in the manner of Robert Newton playing Long John Silver. Great care was taken to impress upon me at all times the infinite knowledge, skill and courage required to sail a cruising yacht, as opposed to a dinghy. I kept expressing my surprise at how much easier everything was on a larger boat.

It went on like that all day, until Dave announced that he had made a command decision not to continue to the Arans, our late departure having made it impossible to reach Kilronan before the pubs closed. Instead, we would divert to Carrigaholt, in the Shannon estuary, where the state of the tide and the closing hours were more in harmony. We did so, and sailing into the estuary Dave showed me how to use a handbearing compass to plot a position on a chart, my introduction to the art of coastal navigation. We berthed the boat at the village pier, then moved on to the pub to wait for Dave's attractive and patient wife to collect us for the drive back to Galway. When we returned to the boat to pick up our gear I discovered another facet of cruising the west coast of Ireland: the rise and fall of the tides. In practice this means that you can tie up nicely level with a pier, trot up to the pub for a few pints and return to find the boat fifteen feet down from its previous level. Negotiating this distance with a full load of Guinness can be tricky. The following week in Dublin I purchased a new item for the inventory of *Pegeen*: a rope ladder. How Dave and Philip had survived for so many seasons without one was beyond me.

The following weekend we journeyed back to Carrigaholt and sailed on to the Arans under spinnaker, with a stiff following breeze which blew us right on to the pubs—all of the pubs—on landing. I forget how many we visited, but the largest had two bars, and the smallest was the

tiny sitting room of an Aran cottage. We lazed about Sunday morning
and then sailed into Galway as the sun set. Everything all those songs
say about the sun setting on Galway Bay is true. The place seems to be
arranged to show the sun at its best—long summer twilights, just
enough cloud to catch and colour the light and the shining waters of the
bay itself. It is best seen from a boat, and it is breathtaking.

All this yachting had quite turned my head. Thoughts of Fireballs
vanished. Visions of cruisers now appeared. I just might be able to
scrape together enough from my two-day-a-week income to buy
something small.

In the meantime there was more sailing with Dave. Next was a new
event, the Round Aran Race, to start from Galway on a Friday evening
and be sailed around all three of the Aran Islands and into Kilronan, a
distance of about sixty miles, with a nice night passage thrown in.

After that came the Galway Bay Sailing Club Regatta. Dave felt that
an event of this stature required a pre-race conference on tactics, and
this was duly held at Moran's (also known as the Weir), a lovely little
thatched pub on the Kilcolgan river, which empties into Galway Bay.
We sailed *Pegeen* up the river, dried her out alongside the pier in front of
the pub, and all concerned, plus a few others, gathered there. I will not
place too much emphasis on the condition of the crew the following
morning; suffice it to say that we ran aground three times on a falling
tide en route to the starting line in Rinville Bay. At one point, half the
crew were over the side in water up to their thighs, pushing *Pegeen*.
Recovery was rapid enough for us to win the coveted *Sonia* cup that
afternoon and we repaired once again to Moran's for a suitable
celebration.

There remained but one weekend before the end of the season, that is
to say, before *Pegeen*'s insurance coverage expired, and it was a
memorable one. Racing was finished and, Philip having allowed his
work to interfere with his sailing, Dave and I took a short cruise.

We sailed down the river and into the bay in about a Force four
breeze, with the full mainsail and the big genoa set. As we entered open
water we looked across to the north of the bay and saw a line of heavy-
looking squalls racing toward us. 'Shall we shorten sail, Skipper?' I
asked.

'Ah, no,' replied Dave, laconically, at his most Irish. 'She'll be all
right.'

The wind freshened quickly and the first puff of the squall, a big one,
struck. There was a loud crack like a rifle shot; Dave was at the helm and
I was sitting near the coachroof bulkhead to keep out of the wind. I
instinctively ducked under the main hatch just in time to see the mast

go, like a felled tree, into the water. The wind was up to about Force seven now, and *Pegeen* wallowed in the troughs as we struggled to get the mast and rigging back aboard. Dave quickly warned me not to start the engine until we were sure the rigging was clear of the propellor. While Dave lashed the badly bent mast and the boom to the deck I got the sails below and bagged them. *Pegeen* was rolling a lot, with no way on, and by the time I got back into the cockpit I was turning a bit green. The engine, bless its heart, chose to start first go, and we motored back toward Galway, the squalls gone and the sun shining again, I trying not to let on that I was queasy. Before I could object Dave had thrust a glass of dry sherry into my hand and was fixing himself a much-deserved gin and tonic. I hadn't wanted the drink, but to my astonishment, at the first sip, my queasiness instantly vanished. A couple of other people have told me that dry sherry works for them, too, and it's a lot more fun than pills.

Pegeen having been safely berthed in the trawler layby, Dave treated me to an end-of-season dinner at the Great Southern Hotel, in the heart of Beautiful Downtown Galway. It had been quite a season for me; I had had the best of both worlds. I had raced the Mirror for a full season and still managed to get quite a lot of time in on *Pegeen* at the tail end. Meanwhile, three weeks before, another event had taken place that was to contribute to a radical redirection of my life. My grandfather, who was a major figure in my life and whom I loved very much, died. It was not a tragic death, for he was eighty-five and quite prepared to die. Well into his late seventies he was doing an hour's callisthenics and running two miles every morning—he had been mowing his lawn when he was struck with his final illness and died only two weeks later. Still, I was sad; my memories of him were sharp and sweet from my earliest childhood, and I miss him even as I write this.

But he was as kind and generous to me in death as he had been in life, and with a riveting suddenness, I realized that I could now afford to buy a small yacht. Then, on the Sunday morning following this realization, I went into the village for the papers and read in the *Observer* that entries were beginning to come in for the 1976 Royal Western/Observer Singlehanded Transatlantic Race.

If I had been a comic strip character, a light bulb would suddenly have appeared above my head.

Book Two
5 On the brink

On the face of it this was a ridiculous idea. In fact, it was entirely possible that it was a ridiculous idea right down to its very toes. My total sailing experience (not counting the week in Maine eight years before, when I was a passenger) consisted of not quite two seasons in a ten-foot ten-inch plywood dinghy and something less than half a season as third hand on a twenty-four-foot bilge keeler. *Pegeen* was the largest boat I had ever set foot on. My total navigation experience consisted of using a handbearing compass maybe three times. I was thirty-six years old and, apart from a little tennis in London and sailing the Mirror, had not had any real exercise in fifteen years. It seemed a meagre chronicle of assets.

But I had others. I was reasonably bright; I had a little money; I had about nineteen months to find a boat, learn to sail it, learn to navigate it and to get fit; and above all, I was, just about as much as any man can be, free. That was a very important consideration.

When I was very young I wanted to get married very badly, but I got over it. I had a couple of close scrapes, mind you, but I managed to stay out of serious trouble. We are all taught that, generally, when between the ages of twenty-one and twenty-five, each of us will meet some Wonderful Person for whom he was destined, then marry, live in a nice house with two cars in the garage, have 2.5 children and live happily ever after. During my twenties, by a process I can only describe as luck, I managed to become gradually disabused of this notion, and by the time I was about thirty it had occurred to me, firstly, that there was a possibility that I might, indeed, never get married; and secondly, that that might not be an unbearably unpleasant way to live. I try to keep an open mind about this, but nothing has yet happened to change it.

So I was free, that is to say, single; neither did I have any burning professional ambition beyond finishing my novel, nor was I burdened with unmanageable debt. My mother being a good business-woman who had just inherited the family business, I had no one to support but myself, and I had been doing that nicely in just two days a week for some time. I was a fortunate man.

Perhaps I was also a slightly insane one. I thought a lot about what my problems would be. I could meet the physical demands, I thought; I could become fit. But what about the emotional demands? Could I spend several weeks alone at sea in a small boat without the top of my head coming off? Well, I had taken a rather cold plunge moving from Knightsbridge in London to Gort in the West of Ireland. It had taken some getting used to, but I now spent the greater part of my time alone, working on the novel or reading, mostly about sailing. The two days a week in Dublin kept me in touch with real life and the opposite sex, but basically, it was a solitary existence.

Most of all, it seemed to me, I faced two things: a problem of organization and an intensive learning experience. There was a lot to bring together in a short time, but I am a compulsive organizer, being a Capricorn; I find it intensely satisfying to bring order out of chaos, and I am good at it. Lately, the only outlet for this compulsion had been the Galway Bay Sailing Club, to the bemusement of its membership. But what about the learning? Quite apart from boat handling technique, there was a considerable amount of academic knowledge to absorb, particularly celestial navigation, which involved mathematics, and I could not count to a hundred without stopping to think. I had been a slightly better than average student at Manchester High School and no better than average at the University of Georgia. Still, I had learned enough about several score of products and companies to be able to write advertising for them; in New York I had become a competent amateur photographer; in London I had learned more than a little about wine. Neither was an uncomplicated subject. If I were enthusiastic about the subject, I could learn.

I wrote to the Royal Western Yacht Club for the rules of the race, and I began to look for a boat. Finding nothing in the Irish newspapers I decided to return from Dublin to Galway the long way and make a few stops. I drove south to Wicklow, stopping at Neil Watson's boatyard. When a boat changes hands in Ireland, Neil Watson often has a hand in the deal. He is the country's most enthusiastic yacht broker and a nice man as well. Neil showed me a variety of craft in his yard. There were a couple of Trappers (not enough interior space, not enough beam), a French Etap (too small), a pair of Irish-built fibreglass boats, called Kerrys (interesting, but freeboard a bit low) and a Comfort 30, a half-ton cruiser-racer, also built in Ireland. This, I thought, was more like it, but it was too expensive, even second-hand. On top of the original cost of the boat there was a lot of extra equipment to be bought. I would have to make do with something smaller.

I drove on to Cork, partly to stop at a favourite country hotel, Ballymaloe House, and partly to see what I could find out about a young New Zealander yacht designer, Ron Holland, about whom I had been reading in the yachting press. He had designed a successful one-tonner, *Golden Apple*, had followed her with a half-tonner, *Golden Shamrock*, and now a production version of *Shamrock* was to be built. Ron Holland was not listed as having a telephone, and I couldn't remember the name of the boatyard which was building his design. It turned out to be Southcoast Boatyard, and I eventually found a small office building, a large shed and the beginnings of some sort of construction behind the office.

In the office I was directed to the foreman, George Bush, whom I found in the shed, deploying workers around the upside-down wooden hull of a boat in building. George, who wears glasses and a permanently astonished look, explained that Ron Holland was in the United States. He showed me the hull he was working on, which was to be the 'plug' around which a mould would be constructed for the new glassfibre boat and gave me a look at *Golden Apple*, which was resting on a cradle near the river. He was very proud of *Golden Apple*, as well he should have been. We talked a bit more, and I left the yard with a clutch of Xeroxed typed pages about the new boat and a promise from George that he would tell Ron Holland of my interest in the boat when he returned from the States. But a production *Golden Shamrock* cost £9,700, and was out of my range.

I continued to West Cork, to Skibbereen, to visit Fastnet Yachts, which turned out to be another tin shed, seemingly in the middle of a farm and nowhere near any water I could see. But there was an astonishing number of boats crammed into this shed, among them a Hurley 24, which interested me. It looked good, and it was within my budget. It was suggested that I have a look at another Hurley 24 in Monasterevin, near Dublin, which had been at the Dublin Boat Show. I did, a few days later, and was very interested.

Not having any objective information about the Hurley, I telephoned *Yachting World* magazine in London and was connected with David Pelly, the assistant editor. He told me that Hurley were a reliable firm who, due to business difficulties not connected with the quality of their product, were in receivership. He spoke well of the 24, calling it a very seaworthy boat for its size and well-designed. I telephoned Hurley's in Plymouth and talked with the sales manager, learning that they had sent the Monasterevin boat to Ireland for the Boat Show, where it had not been sold, and in the meantime, the company had gone into receivership. The receiver was insisting that the boat either be sold soon or brought back to England. I began to smell a genuine, gold-plated bargain.

Back in Galway I noticed in the Royal Ocean Racing Club's magazine, *Sea Horse*, that a Hurley 24 had been sailed in the Round Britain race by Captain Ewan Southby-Tailyour of the Royal Marines. Hurley's gave me his telephone number, and I rang him, slightly uncomfortable because I was not quite sure how to pronounce any of his names. He turned out to be an enthusiast in general and, in particular, about his Hurley 24, *Black Velvet*. He was planning to do the OSTAR in her.

I had in my hand a copy of the rules, which had just arrived in the post. I mentioned a rule that was worrying me. The committee, it said, was unlikely to accept anything under twenty-five feet overall on deck for the race. Ridiculous, said the Captain, they had said the same thing about the Round Britain Race, but he had been accepted. I felt better about it now, and we talked of meeting in London at the Boat Show in January. Nevertheless, after I hung up I wrote to the Committee, asking about the acceptability of the Hurley 24 and reminding them of Captain Southby-Tailyour's performance. I received a courteous note back from the Club Secretary, saying that they knew Ewan Southby-Tailyour well, but he felt it was unlikely that the Committee would accept the Hurley 24. I wrote back and asked for a ruling, remembering that the Committee had, in past times, been known to reconsider an entry.

In the meantime, the negotiations for the Monasterevin boat began to heat up, and I was made an offer which would be very difficult to refuse. I held off, though, waiting for the Committee to meet and rule on the boat. While I was waiting, a letter came from Ron Holland. George Bush had told him that I was interested in a fast cruiser, he said, and he would be happy to talk with me about it.

I had forgotten about Ron Holland's boat in my enthusiasm for the Hurley, and anyway, the Shamrock was out of my price range, but I telephoned him and told him what I was thinking of doing and asked him whether he thought a Shamrock would be a suitable yacht for the OSTAR. He thought it would. It was an easy boat to sail and with its wide beam and high freeboard would be very seaworthy. I asked what modifications, if any, he would make to better suit the boat for its purpose. He'd add a skeg, maybe, to make the boat a bit more directionally stable off the wind and to help the self-steering, which would have to be fitted for the race. I told him I'd think about it.

I still had not made a definite decision to attempt the OSTAR project. I didn't know exactly how much money was going to be available and wouldn't until I went home for the Christmas holidays, and I still hadn't heard from the Committee. Still, I knew I was going to buy some sort of cruising boat, and there were some steps I could take. I heard about a Leonard Breewood, who had started a school of navigation. I rang him up and learned that the full course for the Yachtmaster's Offshore Certificate required three weekends of classroom instruction (forty-eight hours), plus considerable study in between. I signed up for the first weekend of the course.

I drove down to Len Breewood's place in Tralee, a new house on the south shore of Tralee Bay, which he and his wife had built as a combination guest house/sailing and navigation school. It was in a beautiful setting, and Len turned out to be a man of many parts. He had started as a shipwright's apprentice in the Royal Navy and had later taken degrees in both Marine Engineering and Naval Architecture.

He was lecturing in mechanical engineering at a college in Tralee, while building up his sailing school business on the side. A small, wide-eyed man with a dapper beard, he was also an experienced yachtsman and, of course, navigator. My fellow pupil was a native Corkman who was home on leave from his job, which was, improbably, detective inspector in the Hong Kong police force. We spent all day Saturday and Sunday, penetrating the mysteries of compass variation and deviation, chart symbols, tidal streams, the buoyage system, the rule of the road, flashing and occulting lights, passage planning, and two or three dozen other subjects, all brand new to both of us. On Sunday afternoon we plotted a mythical weekend cruise off the south coast. I plotted my course straight through two islands, but apart from my supposed loss of the yacht and my probable fatality, all went well. Sunday night I phoned Ron Holland.

Monday morning I drove to Cork and went to Southcoast Boatyard. I arrived a bit early and occupied my time by taking a ladder around to different boats in cradles on the quay, climbing up to deck level and peering inside. Shortly, I was approached by a rumpled, unshaven figure, wearing jeans and a beat-up sheepskin jacket. Uh, oh, I thought, one of the lads has been sent to tell me not to mess with the boats.

'Hi,' he said, 'I'm Ron Holland.'

6 Things begin to get out of hand

We sat in the sunny dining room of the Grand Hotel in Crosshaven, with a view of the river and, in the distance, the Kelly green hull of *Golden Shamrock*, the prototype, riding at her moorings. We had the place entirely to ourselves, business not being so hot in November, and our very own waiter hovered about. We had tried to get out to Shamrock to have a look at her but couldn't get the club ferry started, so we had repaired to the hotel for some lunch.

Now I was explaining to Ron Holland what I was thinking of doing. I was careful to explain just how little experience I had. It seemed very important not to give him any sort of inflated impression of my state of knowledge. I had, by now, read maybe a dozen books on singlehanding, cruising, yacht design, etc., and it is all too easy to bandy about a few technical terms and give someone the impression that you know more than you do. This is done every day in yacht club bars.

I poured out every thought I had about the race, the kind of boat I thought I needed, what I thought I had to do to get ready, what sort of equipment I would need. He was the first person I had told about this in any detail, and somewhat to my surprise, he seemed not to think I was mad and was actually agreeing with much of what I said. I suppose I had expected him to take a more sceptical view, perhaps even to try to discourage me, but this was not happening. Ron suggested we go to the boatyard and talk with the managing director.

Driving down to Crosshaven before lunch, Ron had pointed out a large Georgian house on the other side of the river and said that he lived in a flat on one side of the house. Now, driving back toward the yard and past the house again, I mentioned that I had often thought that this area would be a nice place to live, what with so much good sailing, but I thought that I could never find as good a situation as I had at Lough

Cutra Castle.

'Let me show you a place we almost took when we came to Cork,' he said. 'It didn't have quite enough room for us, since we're expecting a baby in the spring.'

We drove around to Coolmore, as the house was called, and stopped for a few minutes. Ron's flat was four or five enormous rooms on the south side of the house, and his working space was on the large stair landing. We looked at the original drawings of *Golden Shamrock* and compared them to the production version. The new boat was to have a slightly higher and longer coachroof and a more comfortable interior, but the hull shape was to be identical to that of the prototype.

We met the owner of Coolmore, who looked very much the Master of the Hounds, which, it turned out, he was. He gave us the key to the place Ron wanted to show me, and we drove along a rutted, very muddy road beside the river until we came to a small clearing, where we parked the car. We walked a few yards and came to a lovely old stone cottage right on the banks of the river at a bend called Drake's Pool, so named because Sir Francis Drake is supposed to have eluded the Spanish by hiding there. Because of the double bend in the river they thought it was petering out and went back to search for him in Cork harbour. The Owenboy River has scoured out a deep pool there, and it is a perfect yacht anchorage. There was an empty mooring directly in front of the cottage. We looked inside; a large living room, a large bedroom, a small bedroom, kitchen and bath. The place had been newly plumbed and wired for electricity. I felt a bit giddy; things had begun to move very fast. I looked again at the mooring as we left. It came with the cottage, Ron said.

At the boatyard we encountered the scepticism from its managing director, Barry Burke, that I had half expected from Ron. He wasn't sure that the boat was suitable for a transatlantic passage. Ron said that he'd crossed the Tasman Sea in a similar sized boat. I pointed out that the OSTAR in '72 had been done by David Blagden in a nineteen-foot Hunter and asked if he didn't think his boat would be as strong as a Hunter 19? Ron said he'd give the boat more of a bashing in the 625-mile Fastnet Race than I'd give it in a transatlantic. We talked about making changes to the standard design. Burke was reluctant to slow his production line down with modifications to a standard boat. Pull it off the line, said Ron, and put a couple of men on it. Burke wasn't sure. He asked when I would want the boat. Easter, I said. Impossible, he replied. He'd already sold nine boats. The earliest delivery date would be July 1st. I did some quick mental calculations. The OSTAR rules required a 500-mile qualifying singlehanded cruise no later than three months before the race. I figured that if the boat were ready on July 1st I could just about get her and myself ready for a qualifying cruise before the end of the summer, if I sailed on as many other boats as I could in the spring and early summer. We made a list of the possible modifications to the boat, and Barry promised to let me have an estimate for them. I had hoped that he might agree to some discount, since the boat would undoubtedly receive a lot of attention if it were entered in the OSTAR, and I hoped to do a book about the experience; that would give it even more publicity. Barry didn't seem inclined to give a discount. We left it at that, and I invited Ron to have dinner with me, where we continued our discussion of the yacht and the race. 'What would you change about the boat if you were not building to the Rule?' I asked. (The International Offshore Rule, a rating system so complex that it is only understood by computers, which in turn, explain it to yacht designers and yachting magazines, which publish incomprehensible articles about it.)

Ron looked thoughtful. 'Maybe raise the freeboard a little,' he said. The freeboard is the amount of hull between the deck and the waterline, and, so my reading had told me, was a principal factor in seaworthiness.

'Suppose,' I said, 'we put a two-inch slice of teak between the hull and the deck? That would raise the freeboard and also give me another two inches of headroom in the cabin.' We were talking about how to change the yacht slightly to make it a fast cruiser instead of a flat-out racing boat. We had already talked about sawing the racing-type cockpit out of the glassfibre moulded deck and building a more conventional cruising cockpit with seats and lockers.

'I think that's a rather intelligent solution,' he replied. I glowed at the thought of having contributed an original idea. We talked about what might be squeezed into the interior. Southcoast had hired a Swedish designer to do the interior, and I was considering doing my own layout with Ron's help, since my requirements were different from the man who might race the boat at weekends, then take an occasional family cruise. I wanted no bunks forward in the boat. I wanted a large, empty forepeak for sail stowage and nothing else. It seemed to me that all the other boats I had seen with bunks forward always had the forepeak filled with wet sails anyway, so why have bunks?

Our evening was drawing to a close, and over coffee we had returned to the subject of a novice attempting to learn enough in a short time to sail the race successfully. I outlined what I thought I had to do in the remaining time. Up until now everything had been a big maybe, but I had been encouraged by my practically day-long talk with Ron. Finally, I said, 'I think I can do it.' Ron said, 'I think you can do it, too. I think it's an exciting project, and I'd like to be involved in it.'

I think at that moment the basic decision was made.

Back at Lough Cutra there was a letter waiting from the OSTAR Race Committee. They had decided to accept Ewan Southby-Tailyour's Hurley 24 entry because of his performance in the Round Britain Race but would accept no other Hurley 24's. Had the boat been of that size, but of a more experimental nature, they might have considered it more favourably. I didn't understand that last part, but anyway, my mind was now galloping off on another tack and the Shamrock had replaced the Hurley in my thinking.

Now I began, with no credentials whatever, to become a yacht designer, at least on the inside of the yacht. I pored over the layouts of dozens of other yachts, picking the features I liked best. First of all, since I didn't want berths in the forecabin, that could be smaller and the saloon and toilet areas correspondingly larger. Then I crammed into the space available every feature I had heard about, read about or imagined, and, to my astonishment, it all seemed to fit. A letter arrived from Barry Burke, with an estimate for fitting a skeg, rebuilding the cockpit, raising the decks with my teak sandwich idea and building a custom interior to my specifications. It came to £1600 above the cost of the standard boat. This was daunting, but maybe it could be lowered a bit by negotiation.

I had a telephone conversation with John McWilliam, the Crosshaven sailmaker who had clothed *Golden Apple* and *Golden Shamrock*. He had been out of town during my visit to Cork, but he had since talked with Ron and was enthusiastic about the project. We talked about a possible sail plan and he sent an estimate. Another £1600 or so was added to the budget.

About this time I felt enough committed to the project to begin to let my friends in Galway know what I was thinking. A friend from Dublin came down to Lough Cutra for the weekend, and I invited Harry McMahon and his wife to join us for dinner. At some point during the evening I mentioned, as casually as possible, that I was thinking of buying a Ron Holland half-tonner. The last boat I had mentioned to Harry had been the Hurley, and I hadn't mentioned any plans for it beyond some coastal cruising. 'What would you do with a half-tonner in Galway?' he asked.

I took a deep breath. 'I'm thinking of sailing it in the Observer Singlehanded Transatlantic Race,' I said. Harry looked stunned, his wife burst out laughing. That was to be fairly typical of the reactions of people who knew me as a Mirror helmsman in Galway. I would just have to get used to it.

In early December I went back to see Ron in Cork. He looked at my sketch of the interior and explained, as patiently as he could, that this would not fit, because the sides of the boat did not go straight down, but curved inward. On a cruising boat with fuller 'sections' it might be possible, but not on a hull designed for racing. Together we drew up a compromise of what *might* be possible. He did, however, agree with my idea of pushing the saloon bulkhead (wall) forward by making the forecabin smaller. Ron pulled out the drawings of a three-quarter-tonner he had designed for production in glassfibre, called the Quest 32. The company who were to manufacture it had gone under. We all agreed that it was a great pity that it would not now be built. Ron was at a stage of his career when he needed several boats in series production, just about the only way a yacht designer can make any real money.

Ron Holland was born and grew up in New Zealand, sailing from an early age. After secondary school he served an apprenticeship in boat building and, as a part of that, took some drafting and design courses. He then went to the United States and worked in California for a well-known designer, Gary Mull, and later, in Florida, for Charley Morgan of Morgan Yachts. He met the sailing-oriented family of Carlins there and married their daughter Laurel. In 1973, sailing his own boat, he won the world quarter-ton championships. The boat was called *Eyghtene* (after the Australian pronunciation of eighteen). After the world championships Ron was living aboard the little twenty-four-footer in the Hamble river in England when he was approached by a young Cork businessman about designing a one-tonner. Ron and Laurel came to Cork to talk about it, fell in love with Ireland and stayed. *Golden Apple* performed brilliantly but erratically in the world one-ton championships in 1974, but she was obviously the fastest boat there and caught the attention of everybody, including the yachting press, and Ron's reputation soared.

Back in Cork, Southcoast Boatyard, which had built *Golden Apple*, asked him to design a half-tonner to be built in time for the world half-ton championships at La Rochelle, in France. The boat, the original *Golden Shamrock*, was rushed to completion and arrived in La Rochelle barely in time for the first race. Because of a stretching of rigging which had occurred on the passage to France, and the lack of time to replace it, *Shamrock* was dismasted in the first race. Somehow, another mast was obtained immediately, and the crew stayed up all night rigging the boat. After that, she performed spectacularly, even in survival conditions, and the decision was made to put the design into series production in glass fibre. Now Ron had another one-off design, a two-tonner intended for the Irish Admiral's Cup team, and the biggest boat he had yet designed. This, he hoped, would be as important a boat as *Golden Apple*, but he still wanted more designs in series production. The dying of the Quest 32 was a blow.

In Cork I also met John McWilliam, the sailmaker, and had another talk with Barry Burke at Southcoast. I also had a talk with Ron's landlord, and told him I was very interested in the cottage. He seemed amenable to having me there.

A few days later, as my Aer Lingus flight took off from Shannon Airport, headed for New York, then Georgia and the Christmas holidays, a broad plan had come together for the project: move to Cork in February, study navigation all winter and sail during the spring on any boat whose skipper would have me; the boat would start building May 1st and be launched July 1st; then sail her intensively, going out to southwest France and northwest Spain or perhaps even the Azores with friends, then sail back to Crosshaven, singlehanded, for my qualifying cruise. (I wanted to sail more than the minimum five hundred miles, hoping that a longer qualifying cruise would count with the Race Committee against my inexperience.)

The cottage would have, within a five-mile radius, the boatyard, the designer and the sailmaker. Both Ron and John McWilliam had promised me as much time as they could spare in tuning the boat and helping me to learn to sail her. The only big question mark was the money, and that would be resolved, one way or the other, when I arrived in the States.

It seemed a very neat programme. I could only hope that, in my ignorance, I had not made it too neat, had not failed to take some hugely important factor into account which, when it emerged, would wreck the whole project. If my own funds wouldn't cover the cost, then there was the possibility of commercial sponsorship. I felt that, if I had to, I could probably do a better job than most in attracting commercial attention, since I had spent all of my working life in advertising, dealing on a daily basis with the sort of people I would have to approach.

The novel would have to wait a couple of years, but then, a novel can always wait, as any novelist can tell you.

The project was all there, in outline, I could do nothing more until January, except think about it. And until January I would think about nothing else.

7 Things begin to gel

Manchester, Georgia, is a town of about six thousand people, located about seventy miles south of Atlanta, the state capital. It is, perhaps, 250 miles from the nearest body of salt water, and the populace is not made up of sailing enthusiasts. A boat is something you row or propel with an outboard motor and is used in the catching of large mouth bass and catfish. To my mother, who is not interested in fishing, boats mean even less.

Dot, which is short for Dorothy and is what I have called her ever since I learned to talk, did not quite seem to get it when I explained to her what I planned to do. I spread out the plans for the boat and explained it all again. Still, I don't think the penny dropped until a few days later. We were sitting in her car in a supermarket parking lot, about to drive home with the groceries, when she asked suddenly, 'Are you really going to do this?'

'Do what?' I asked. We had not discussed the subject since the day before.

'Sail that little boat across the Atlantic Ocean by yourself.'

'Yes.'

Gene Spain, our family life insurance man, happened to be strolling through the parking lot at that moment. Dot rolled down the car window. 'Gene, I want you to come by the house,' she said. 'I want to talk to you about some insurance.' Gene forgot about his grocery shopping.

A few minutes later the two of them had worked out the details of a fairly hefty policy on my life, over my strenuous protests. 'What do I need with insurance?' They ignored me.

'Do you want double indemnity?' asked Gene. 'There's only a small additional premium.'

'How much is treble indemnity?' asked my mother.

After that she seemed resigned to the idea. She learned long ago that it is difficult to talk me out of something I'm excited about. We met with the family attorney to sort out my grandfather's estate, and I discovered to my astonishment that my estimate of what he had left me was short by half. Now I could afford the Shamrock and all the necessary equipment.

I had to cut my stay short by a few days in order to get to London in time for the tail end of the London Boat Show. I stopped off in New York for a day and managed to see half-a-dozen old friends, then flew to Shannon. Harry McMahon met me the next day at Lough Cutra, and we drove to Cork to catch the ferry to England. But first I had two things to accomplish in Cork.

First, I went to Southcoast Boatyard and, after some discussion, worked out a deal with Barry Burke: I would buy the standard boat at the full price, then the boatyard would carry out any alterations I wanted and maintain the boat until the start of the race at cost for materials and at cost plus ten per cent for labour. The boatyard would also obtain any extra gear I required at trade prices. We signed the contract; Barry gave me a letter outlining the alteration and maintenance and equipment agreement, and I gave him a £500 deposit. We agreed on half the remaining price being paid at the time of moulding, May 1st, and the remainder on launching, July 1st. Harry witnessed the contract. I was delighted with the arrangement and felt it was a good one for both of us. Barry seemed to think so, too.

Next, I called at Coolmore, to finalize arrangements about the cottage. By noon the next day we were at the London Boat Show.

We were like Babes in Toyland. Galway had no well-equipped chandleries and Dublin, at that time, was not much better. When we wanted a piece of equipment a complicated mail-order procedure was involved, and often a battle with the transport services and customs. Now, spread before us, were two huge floors packed with everything anyone could possibly want for a boat, from the smallest cleat to the tallest mast. There were only two and a half days left of the show, and I had to buy or at least research virtually every piece of equipment that would be needed for my yacht. I bought a sextant, instruments, a hand-bearing compass, a VHF radio-telephone, clothing, a wetsuit, books, and much else from a long list. I carefully researched liferafts and inflatable dinghies, emergency radio transmitters, self-steering and electronics. Whenever possible I approached manufacturers about possible discounts on equipment.

On my return there were still one or two things to do before the move to Cork. I talked to some of the cruising people in the club, and we agreed to ask Len Breewood to come up to Galway for three weekends during the winter to teach the Yachtmaster's Offshore navigation course. Len agreed to come for one weekend a month starting in February.

The other thing was to talk with Commander Bill King. Bill King is a retired Royal Navy submarine commander, in fact, the only submarine commander in any navy, he believes, who started World War II in command of a submarine and who was still alive at the end of it all. He had one hell of a war and has written about it in his own excellent book, *Adventure in Depth*. After the war, annoyed by the Royal Navy's recalcitrance in adopting modern methods, he spent some years in ocean racing and sailing his own boat, then went to farm in County Galway and remained there in contentment with his wife, the writer Anita Leslie, until the late 1960s. Then he began planning a long-held dream to sail around the world, singlehanded, non-stop. The *Sunday Times*, hearing about this, offered a £5,000 prize and a trophy, the Golden Globe, for the first man to complete the voyage. Bill's boat, designed by Angus Primrose, partner of Bill's wartime and postwar ocean racing friend, the legendary John Illingworth, and by Colonel 'Blondie' Hasler, who designed the Chinese Junk rig, was named *Galway Blazer II*. Bill set off alone, opposing Robin Knox-Johnston, Bernard Moitessier and others, to race around the world, alone, without stopping.

About a thousand miles southwest of Capetown, South Africa, *Blazer* was rolled over in 120 knots of wind and dismasted. Bill sailed her to Capetown under a jury rig and shipped her back to England for repairs. Those completed, he set off again, and had to put into Gibraltar because of rigging problems. The yacht was once again returned to England, and he set off again. By this time, Robin Knox-Johnston was, beyond doubt, the winner of the race, Moitessier having continued to sail on to Tahiti after rounding Cape Horn, and the others having turned back or lost their boats. But Bill King was determined to complete his voyage for his own personal satisfaction.

On his third attempt, he was sailing two hundred miles off Western Australia when the yacht was attacked by a Great White shark and badly holed. In a magnificent act of seamanship and personal courage, Bill temporarily plugged the hole and sailed into port. Repairs completed, he finished his voyage without another stop, arriving back in Galway in early 1973, shortly after I had moved there. I had met him socially once or twice and had told him of my long range plan of doing some deep water sailing. He invited me to come and talk with him about it.

At the Boat Show I had been delighted to find that the Multihull

Offshore Cruising and Racing Association (MOCRA) had organized a race to Horta, in the Azores, for August 1975, the very time I had been thinking of sailing there. I signed up immediately. Now, I went to see Bill King and asked if he'd like to come. He had not sailed at all since returning from his circumnavigation, but two years had passed and he must have been getting itchy for the sea. He accepted immediately. He would sail out with me and one or two other people and would hitch a ride home on another yacht while I sailed back singlehanded. He also offered to come to Cork when the yacht was building and share his enormous experience. I was delighted.

That accomplished, I packed my things into a furniture van and moved to Drakes Pool Cottage, Coolmore, Carrigaline, Co. Cork.

Drake's Pool Cottage. The mooring is right in front.

8 Waiting for Spring

Driving back to the cottage from Carrigaline, about three miles away and the closest village, it occurred to me how isolated I would be at Drake's Pool. The road to Coolmore wasn't really on the way to anywhere, except Currabinny, and that just barely qualified as anywhere. I thought the isolation would be good for work on the novel, but not so good for social life. Still musing on my remove from the rest of the world, I arrived at the cottage to find a *Watchtower* magazine on my doorstep. It seemed that, to the Jehovah's Witnesses, nobody was isolated.

The following day I was sitting among my unpacked books, typing a letter, when two pretty girls appeared at the front door. Terrific! Not so isolated, after all! They turned out to be the Jehovah's Witnesses. Still . . . I invited them in and we got into a hot religious discussion. I was annoyed by the ease with which they backed up their convictions with seemingly ambiguous quotes from the scriptures, so I dug a Bible from one of the tea chests and fenced with them for a bit. I scored no points in this debate. There was always a ready scriptural reference, there to be taken literally. Finally, I asked how they felt about sex—outside marriage, I meant. Oh, no. Against the rules, and a couple of suspect verses were quoted. I asked if they believed in a just God. Oh, yes, certainly. Well, I said, I didn't think a just God would require me to remain celibate just because I had happened not to get married. They made an excuse and left.

Worth Newnham, my new landlord, and his wife turned up with a gift bag of turf for the fireplace and stayed for a drink. I asked where I might get a bookcase built in the neighbourhood. Books follow me about relentlessly wherever I go, multiplying steadily. When I had left London for Ireland I had given most of my library away, but the few I had brought with me (only about four packing cases full) had done their multiplication trick. The cottage would not be livable until I got them out of the boxes and into a bookcase, a large bookcase. Worth suggested I talk with Nick Roe, who was living on an old trawler on a mooring in front of the cottage, rebuilding it. Nick Roe was to become a very important part of my project, before it was all done.

Nick stopped by later with his brother and girl friend. They were all living on the boat, which was quite quite large. Nick was very busy with his work, but he agreed to build the bookcase for me.

Gradually, things got unpacked, and I settled in. Ron dropped by now and then. I visited the boatyard, where the new factory for the series production was now complete and the first hull and deck was being moulded. The factory looked good, and I felt more confident about the building of the boat. I had conversations about alterations to the boat with the production manager and with George Bush, who would be in charge of the extra work.

On the sponsorship front, I started with the *Irish Times*, perhaps the best of the Irish national newspapers. I had a meeting in Dublin with a member of their management and their advertising agency, and they expressed interest in sponsoring the project, perhaps in concert with another Irish company, yet to be found. I started looking. I tried Guinness, first. They seemed a logical place to start, and through an acquaintance, they gave a logical reason for not sponsoring; they had cut back on all but existing sponsorship; they had just turned down a pub in Waterford for a trophy for their darts championship. They could hardly turn them down, then have the lads see on TV that they were sponsoring a yacht, could they?

To save time in explaining what I was doing, I wrote a description of the project and had copies run off. I began sending these to prominent Irish companies, since I intended being an Irish entry. A rule of the race stated that the nationality of the entry would be the nationality of the skipper. In December, when I had written to the Committee formally reserving a place in the race, pending the qualifying cruise, I explained that, although I was an American I had lived for some time in Ireland and had learned to sail there from Irish yachtsmen on Irish boats, and I requested that an exception be made and I be allowed to become an Irish entry. I had received a letter from the Royal Western Yacht Club saying that would be fine. Shortly after reserving my place I noticed an article in the *Observer* by yachting correspondent Frank Page, giving the number of entries by nationality. No Irish entry had been mentioned, and I dropped him a note saying that there would be an Irish entry, and since I was looking for Irish sponsorship, could he please say so sometime in his newspaper?

My race number of twenty-four was also confirmed. This number might pose something of a problem, since it had to be displayed on the sails, hull and deck, and I was also entered for the MOCRA Azores race, which might assign me a different number. The problem was solved by asking MOCRA to make me entry number twenty-four in their race, and by asking the Irish Yachting Association for the sail number IR 24; both requests were granted.

The new two-tonner, which would be called *Irish Mist II*, was quickly taking shape at Southcoast. When introduced to Archie O'Leary, the owner, I offered to crew on any delivery trips he might be making when his own racing crew were not available. He promised to keep me in mind.

I found myself extremely busy, although my boat had not yet begun building. I was hustling about, ordering equipment and trying to ensure that it all arrived in time for the launching of the yacht; I was working hard on the sponsorship problem; I was writing to manufacturers, asking for discounts.

Also, I was negotiating with a publisher about a book describing the project. Ron was working on a book for Stanford Maritime, and he and his editor stopped by the cottage for a drink. After hearing about what I was doing, he expressed interest, and eventually we signed a contract. Finally, I still wanted to do some advertising work in Dublin.

I was trying to do all of this with no help whatsoever from the Irish Department of Posts and Telegraphs. In Galway it had taken me fourteen months to wrench a telephone from their grasp, and they had assured me that, as an existing subscriber, when I moved to Cork there would be no problem getting a telephone immediately. (The word 'immediately' has no meaning in Ireland. It's just a word.) However, when I arrived in Cork, although my application had preceded me by more than a month, nothing was happening. Finally, after weeks of telephone conversations (they never, never actually wrote any letters, although I would periodically receive a printed form telling me that my problem was being dealt with) they finally told me that nobody who lived more than a quarter of a mile from an existing telephone line could be provided with service, and that I lived 175 yards beyond that distance. Although I clawed my way through what seemed like the entire Irish Civil Service, the situation remained frozen for months.

Other communication systems were, however, working. One bright Sunday morning I awoke to find that, having left the reversing lamp on my car on all night, the battery was completely dead. Being some distance from a telephone, I had another idea. The VHF radio-telephone which I had bought at the London Boat Show was a self-contained one, having its own power supply. Technically, the radio was not supposed to be operated except on the yacht, and only after having been licensed. The boat did not even exist yet, and I had not even applied for a license, but I got out the list of Irish coastal stations and the instructions for transmission procedure. I studied them for a few minutes and then switched on the radio.

'Cobh Radio, Cobh Radio, Cobh Radio (the Cork Harbour station) this is Woodsmoke, Woodsmoke, Woodsmoke (a tentative name for the yacht). Do you read me?' Silence for two minutes, the instructions said. Then if no reply, try again. I tried again.

I jumped about a foot when a clear voice said, 'Woodsmoke, Woodsmoke, Woodsmoke, this is Cobh Radio, Cobh Radio, Cobh Radio, what is your position? Over.'

'Cobh Radio, I'm at Drake's Pool, uh, ashore, uh, and I have a problem with my car. I wonder if you could possibly telephone the AA for me? Over.'

Silence. He probably didn't think he was hearing properly. Then he came back. 'Woodsmoke, we don't ordinarily do that sort of thing, but we're not too busy right now, and I've been in that position myself. How will the AA find you? Over.'

'I'm at Drake's Pool Cottage . . .'

'Cottage!' He interrupted. After all, this was supposed to be a ship to shore radio.

'Ah, yes, there's this cottage, and my car is parked there.' I gave him the complicated directions for finding me and we signed off.

An hour later an AA man appeared, scratching his head and saying that he'd never had a call like this one before. I had half expected the police, but a minute or two later the car was started. I never used the VHF ashore again, though.

The Dublin Boat Show rolled around, and I used the trip to Dublin to check on what was happening with the *Irish Times*. Nothing, apparently. However, Exide had agreed to donate the batteries for the boat. It was the first equipment I had been given, and was a lift to the spirits. The Dublin Show seemed small after the London one, but it was interesting, and I bought an outboard motor for the dinghy and a few small things.

Back at Southcoast, the first deck went onto the first hull of the new series. It was the first glimpse I had of anything like the complete boat, and I was impressed with what a pretty craft she was going to be. The first and third boats in the series were being sent out unfinished, in kit form, but the second boat, a bright red one which would be finished in the factory was getting underway, and I was looking forward to seeing it take shape.

Then Fred vanished. He was grown now, but still very much the puppy at heart, and he missed the dogs and children at Lough Cutra, especially the children. He had taken to walking the mile or so to the main gate of Coolmore, where a group of small kids gathered to play, and one night, he didn't come home. To make matters worse, his collar and name tag had disappeared the day before, so nobody would know where he came from. As the days passed with no sign of him I took to driving around the countryside looking for him. He had been stolen twice as a puppy, but recovered, and I was increasingly worried about him. He was the only company I had in the cottage, and good company he was, always making me laugh, bringing me sticks to throw into the river for him to retrieve. He liked swimming better than walking, being a Labrador. I put notices up in the post offices in the surrounding villages. He was seen at Ringaskiddy, then Currabinny, then Douglas, eight miles away. There were apparently a lot of Golden Labradors about. Since I didn't have a phone, Ron was taking the calls, and they were coming in at the rate of two or three a day. I got one from Kanturk, twenty miles away, but it turned out to be a different Lab. Finally, I put an ad in the *Cork Examiner*, and someone in Douglas called. They had had a strange Labrador about for days. I went to Douglas. It was Fred. He had been gone for two weeks. The minute he was home he had a stick in his mouth, ready for his swim. He got a new collar and ID tag the same day.

Fred, bored with chasing sticks, takes on a tree.

9 Organize, organize, organize

In late March we had the second of our navigation classes in Galway, and I managed to get a lot into the weekend. I had dinner with Harry and Lorna McMahon, and although Bill King was away (skiing), his wife, Anita, joined us. What a delightful woman she is. We talked about her best-selling book, *Jenny,* based on the life of Winston Churchill's mother. Anita's grandmother was Jenny's sister, and Anita had known Lady Randolph Churchill as a child. The television series based on the book was running at the time, and talk centered on that. She mentioned that Bill was looking forward eagerly to the Azores trip. I asked Harry to come as well, but he was doubtful whether he'd be able to manage the time. I had already invited Ewan Southby-Tailyour, but he wasn't sure whether the Royal Marines would give him time to do the Azores race and the OSTAR in successive years.

Our navigation class went well, and we agreed to spend our final weekend, in April, cruising to the Aran Islands and back, putting our new-found knowledge into practice.

Back in Cork, it was time to place my order for sails, and John McWilliam and I sat down to discuss this. Getting John McWilliam to sit down is no small feat. He is the only person I met during the whole of my stay in Ireland who is visibly energetic about his work.

John McWilliam is a northerner, from the Six Counties, and after engineering school did a spell with the RAF, doing individual aerobatics with the famous Red Arrows stunt team at air shows. After that, he did an apprenticeship with the Australian sailmaker, Rolly Tasker, in his Hong Kong loft, then opened a Tasker branch in Ireland. By the time I arrived, he had gone out on his own, making his sails on the main floor of an old stone mill on the hill behind Crosshaven, and living in a handsome flat on the top floor.

Visiting the McWilliam Sailmakers' loft is an experience. You can feel the glass vibrating before you even open the door, and inside, sound strikes with a physical force. There is a suped-up stereo system driving a series of huge speakers, and the noise which comes out is overpowering to all but the demented teenyboppers with whom John McWilliam shares his musical taste. Through two more sets of sliding doors and into the loft proper, one comes upon Mr McWilliam, loping about the varnished floor, carpet slippers on his feet, foam rubber taped to his knees, with a grace of movement not seen since the actor known as Stepinfetchit plied the Silver Screen. John moves much faster, though, and constantly.

John is also very bright, and a first rate man on a racing yacht. He is probably the only one of the world's top three or four sailmakers who still cuts every sail himself, assisted only by his right-hand man and a harem of local girls, who, even while bent over their sewing machines, giggle and blush constantly. John makes up for being in an out-of-the-way place by delivering his sails to customers all over the British Isles and Europe in a twin-engined Piper Apache, the flying of which gives him enormous pleasure. He probably gives his customers a more personal and more effective service than some sailmakers located in hotbeds of sailing activity like the south coast of England. He claims to charge less, too, and his sails are nearly as good as he says they are.

The sail plan we worked out for my boat was made up of a mainsail, a large genoa (foresail), a number two genoa (slightly smaller than the large one), a medium-weight spinnaker for all-round use, a floater spinnaker for very light winds and a smaller 'starcut' spinnaker for reaching and for running in heavy winds. (Later we dropped the starcut, because I realized I wasn't about to set a spinnaker, singlehanded, in strong winds.) There would be no smaller headsail than the number two genoa, because I intended to reef that sail rather than change down to a smaller one. This would be done by virtue of a device called a Dynafurl. It works this way: the sail, instead of being set on an ordinary wire forestay, is set on a grooved, solid rod forestay, called a Twinstay. In ordinary, crewed racing, a sail can be set on this stay while another one is still drawing, giving an advantage over conventional sail changing. The Dynafurl consists of two swivels, one at the top of the stay and one at the bottom. When reefing the sail, a rope is pulled and the sail wraps itself tightly around the forestay, displaying progressively smaller area. It can be reefed right down to storm jib size in this fashion.

My reason for choosing this system was twofold: (1) I reasoned that in a 3000-mile race, an awful lot of time could be spent changing sails in changeable conditions, and the boat would be slowed during sail changes; (2) If the only sail change I had to make was from the number one genoa to the number two genoa, this would keep me off the foredeck in heavy weather, when it can be a very dangerous place. My only sail change would be made in less than fifteen knots of wind.

The mainsail, instead of having roller reefing, where the sail is rolled up around the boom, would have slab reefing, in which the sail is simply tied to the boom by a row of cringles (eyes) sewn across the sail. This would be faster singlehanded, and the sail would set better as well.

Later, we would add two other sails to the wardrobe; one, a duplicate number two genoa, so that twin headsails could be set when running in fresher winds, and so that I would have a spare for my principal working sail. Twin headsails are easier to control than a spinnaker and have self-steering properties, too, which would be a help in strong winds. The other addition would be a drifter, or very light large genoa, made of nylon. This would help considerably when beating or reaching in very light winds. Much later, the need for a storm jib would present itself, but I'll get to that later.

The sails ordered and a delivery date promised to coincide with the boat's launching, I set about selecting other gear. I chose the well-known Hasler Windvane self-steering system. I must admit I chose it with a minimum of research. Mike Ellison, of the Amateur Yacht Research Society, which had done much research, recommended it, and so did Ron Holland. The difficult decision to make was whether to order the small or medium size of the unit. My boat fell in a grey area where the small unit might be big enough and might not. But the larger unit was twice as heavy and twice as expensive, so I took the chance and went for the smaller one. I would not know until the boat was launched whether I had made the right decision, and I was plagued by doubt.

I chose the Avon four-man liferaft and the Avon Redcrest inflatable dinghy as my tender. Both were well-proven, and I had been impressed by Avon quality at the London Boat Show. Liferaft stowage was going to be a problem, because even a four-man raft is rather bulky, and no place had been designed into the Shamrock for it, a mistake, I felt, and one which I communicated to Ron on more than one occasion. I chose Brookes & Gatehouse electronic instruments, simply because, from everything I could gather from every source I could find, they were considered to be the finest in the world. I ordered their Hornet unit, which combines, in one control box, wind speed, wind direction, magnified wind direction (a fine display for beating to windward), water speed and distance covered. To this I added the Hound water speed amplifier, which gives a finer display of small changes in speed and is invaluable for fine sail trimming.

I also, after much soul searching, ordered the B & G Horatio unit, which offers several functions. Once a course is set into an electronic compass on the deckhead, steering can be done by keeping a needle on a dial straight up, instead of steering a compass course, which demands more concentration and is more tiring. The unit also has an off-course alarm, which can be set for either twenty or forty degrees, important when the boat is under self-steering and will change direction automatically if the wind direction changes. Finally, there is a constant digital readout of the number of miles sailed to either port or starboard of a set course. This would be valuable when setting a course when about to go to sleep. On awaking, I would know how far off course I might have sailed. Horatio was an expensive piece of equipment, costing as much as the complete Hound, but I felt I might genuinely need it.

I also chose the B & G Homer/Heron radio receiver and radio direction finding compass, and the shortwave converter for the radio, which would enable me to pick up radio time signals at sea.

To the Brookes & Gatehouse equipment I added the ubiquitous Seafarer depth sounder (at the suggestion of B & G, because I wanted to economize), and the Seavoice VHF, already mentioned, made by the same company. (I later exchanged the self-contained model for the ordinary model, because I was having difficulty finding room for the extra bulk of the first unit.)

Finally, I added, as a back-up radio receiver, the American Zenith Transoceanic Portable, probably the best of its kind, and a Philips car stereo radio/tape player, purely for entertainment. At home I am never without music playing, and I would have missed this terribly at sea.

That was a lot of electronic and electrical gear, but it all got used. I have always had a thing about being well-equipped, and the boat would be evidence to this part of my character. In defence, I must say that I felt my lack of experience made electronic help all the more important. A life-long sailor might guess at the windspeed or direction accurately, but I could not. I felt I needed all the help I could get. This feeling, it turned out, was entirely correct.

I had to choose an engine as well. The choice was between the Yanmar 12 and the Faryman 12 diesels, the Faryman having hydraulic drive. The Yanmar has a good reputation, and I was offered a nice discount on it, but I chose the Faryman because of its compact size and the versatility of installation of the Hydromarine Hydraulic Drive. This equipment is manufactured in Ireland, and Hydromarine offered me, at no extra cost, a heavy duty unit more suitable for running for long periods without a load, as when charging batteries. They were later to give unstintingly of technical help and advice.

On March 27th, Laurel Carlin Holland gave birth to a daughter, Kelly, much to the astonishment of everyone, since triplets, at a minimum, had been expected. Ron was completely bemused by the idea of being a father, and we had a celebratory dinner at Ballymaloe.

My social situation took a turn for the better when a letter came from Ann O'Donahue, a London friend, in response to an invitation issued in January. She would be arriving in early April for a visit. I was looking forward to that. The only people I knew in Cork were my designer, sailmaker and boatbuilder, none of them very pretty.

Ann arrived on Monday afternoon and we renewed our acquaintance over dinner at Arbutus Lodge, Cork's best restaurant and, many think, Ireland's. Having Ann about the place made an enormous difference. We had the Hollands and Barry and Mary Burke over for dinner and, confirming conversations we had been having, Barry promised to mould my boat next, making it number seven instead of ten. She would be launched, said Barry, around June 1st. This was an enormous relief to me. The red boat was only now being completed, and I had been increasingly worried about having the boat ready for the Azores race. Now I would have a month more to sail her than planned!

The red boat was finally launched on April 11th. In the water she was very pretty, and we arranged to go sailing on her with Ron and John McWilliam on Sunday.

We were joined by Harold Cudmore, a dinghy sailor, now becoming a helmsman in offshore racing, and a non-stop talker about sailing, Cork and anything Irish. The boat was a delight to sail. I was astonished at how quickly she tacked. We sailed about Cork harbour, while Ron ceaselessly tuned the rigging and McWilliam admired his sails. Ron never seems to stop moving on a boat. He is everywhere, dressed in a pair of white painter's overalls, or something equally awful, completely indifferent to what the fashionable yachtsman is supposed to be wearing, and always with tools in his hands. Sometimes he will deign to wear a battered pair of seaboots. Ron seems vaguely uncomfortable in anything new, or even pressed.

McWilliam, on the other hand, is extremely neat, though not given to fashion, as such. He always seems ironed and starched, even on a boat. I think his wife presses him before he leaves the house.

Cudmore, a rangy fellow with a lot of thick, red hair and a native capacity for Guinness, enjoys giving instructions in a manner which manages to be, at once, quick and easy. Both Ron and Harold are good teachers on a boat, each having a large fund of knowledge on every detail of the sailing of a yacht, and a willingness to share it. McWilliam, on the other hand, although possessed of at least as much information, seems to assume that anyone who is over the age of seven has a native understanding of everything that makes a yacht work, and an equal knowledge of things mechanical. Once, when I interrupted him, puzzled by a discourse on load factors or something, he said to me, 'You know, it's good training for me to talk to you about things like this; your mind is so . . . so . . . .' 'Unsullied by knowledge?' I volunteered. He grinned. 'That's it,'

Everything about this first sail in a Shamrock was an eye-opener for me. First of all, it was, at this point in my experience, the largest boat I had ever sailed on; secondly, it was my introduction to what my own boat would be like, and I was both a little awed by the height of the mast and the sail area, and relieved, in that the yacht didn't seem unmanageable. Ann, who says of her ability on a boat, 'I do what I'm told', was enjoying herself, too. At least nobody was yelling at her. She tells of a sail down the Channel once with a male companion who became Captain Bligh on a boat. She abandoned ship in Weymouth and took a train back to London.

Sailing back to moorings in front of the Yacht Club, Cudmore gave me a real workout. Harold would rather sail any time than use an engine (I saw him sail up to a mooring under spinnaker once, in a riverful of moored yachts), and he decided we would short tack up the river, against the tide. Ron and McWilliam quickly found something to do on the foredeck, and I had to man both winches, with Ann tailing the sheets. I was wiped out by the time we reached the mooring, and after three months on my exercise programme. It occured to me that had I tried that in January I would have collapsed after the first four or five tacks.

Back at the Royal Cork, we ran into Hugh Coveney in the bar and got into a discussion of boats' names. Hugh's *Golden Apple* name came from Yeats . . . 'The golden apples of the sun and the silver apples of the moon . . .' The 'Golden' handle had continued with *Golden Shamrock*, and I thought I'd like to keep it going, combined with something Irish, but a bit more elegant than Shamrock. The harp is the Irish national symbol, and that of the Royal Cork Yacht Club as well. *Golden Harp* seemed a good possibility. Hugh liked that, and I think from that time on, though I thought about other names, the yacht, in my own mind, became *Golden Harp*.

Ann flew back to London that afternoon, and I was alone again. Still, my boat was about to begin building, and I was about to make my first passage of the season and my first to England. *Golden Apple* had been sold, and Hugh Coveney had invited me to sail on the delivery trip.

10 My first golden cruise

The next two weeks were mostly occupied with final meetings about the moulding of the boat. I think we had at least three final meetings. I was beginning to have doubts about some of the modifications planned for the boat. First, I abandoned the idea of replacing the whole cockpit and decided just to make the existing one deeper. Then I was talked out of that, because of doubts about the cockpit draining properly when heeled. Finally, George talked me out of raising the decks with the teak sandwich idea. He was concerned about the possibility of leaks around the hull/deck join. I gave in on the custom interior, too. I would accept the Swede's standard interior and simply add extra stowage space.

A letter came from Mike Ellison of the Amateur Yacht Research Society, who was helping to organize the Azores race. When Harry McMahon and Ewan Southby-Tailyour had not been able to get enough free time to do the race, I had told Mike I'd consider taking a girl crew, which the committee had suggested entrants do. Now Mike had two candidates for me, and the following day I received a letter from one of them, Shirley Clifford. She sounded fine, but she was married to Richard Clifford, a Royal Marine officer who had done the last OSTAR, and I wrote her a frank letter explaining that I had not expected inquiries from a married lady, and that I didn't want any angry Marines buzzing about. I didn't, either.

Golden Apple departed about one o'clock on a Friday afternoon, Hugh Coveney having come down to provision and fuel us. The rest of the crew were Ian Hannay, skipper, an English airline pilot and, as it turned out, a former British Olympic helmsman in the Dragon class; Richard Edwards, an English medical student; and Killian Bush, George's son. Killian worked at the yard and had crewed on *Apple* the year before. I'd had some sort of mild bug since the day before and was feeling rotten, so as soon as we set sail at Roche's Point, at the mouth of Cork Harbour, I turned in until time for my watch. It annoyed me to feel poorly at the beginning of a trip to which I had so looked forward; it was my first sail out of sight of land.

I was awakened later by the sound of the engine starting. It was a sound I would grow to hate during the next three days. The wind had been light when we set sail, and now it had dropped to nothing. Motoring on a Ron Holland one-off racing yacht is not like motoring on anything else. Instead of the purr of an engine, muffled by soundproofing, we had a deafening chug, muffled only by a panel of sailcloth between the quarter berth and the engine. Soundproofing is too heavy to be used on a superfast Holland design. We motored on through the late afternoon and into the evening, picking up, at some point, an exhausted pigeon who perched on a spreader, hunkered his head down and fell into an apparently dreamless sleep, stirring himself from time to time to shit on the deck below.

Dawn came slowly, and we found ourselves motoring onward in a haze that made it impossible to judge distance. The sun shone weakly through it. The effect was one of being anchored in one place with the engine running, there was so little sensation of movement in the haze. By late afternoon things had cleared enough to sight Land's End, my first landfall in a yacht, and that was exciting. That lower, left hand corner of England was abeam by 20.00 hours, and I turned in after my three hour watch, looking forward to nine uninterrupted hours of sleep. Motoring was curiously tiring, and I still felt rotten. I was awakened by Hannay at 03.00 after only six hours sleep and told that I was on watch. (Often on a yacht when racing, or when cruising in heavy weather, the skipper and/or the navigator does not take a watch, but saves himself and is awakened if there are problems.)

It was now clear and very cold (it was only April, remember) with a huge full moon lighting everything through the haze. As I took the helm, Richard gave me the course and said he hadn't sighted the Lizard light and thought we had probably passed it in the fog, earlier. I settled down in my long underwear, jeans, two sweaters, offshore jacket, lined mittens and my Balaclava. The Balaclava was the best idea I'd ever had, I thought, keeping me nice and warm inside my jacket's hood.

Half-an-hour later I sighted two flashing lights slightly off the starboard bow. This was very peculiar, according to the ship's light patterns I had studied in the yachtmaster's course. A larger ship will have two mast lights, one high, aft and one lower, forward. But they do not flash. The only thing that flashes is a lighthouse or a buoy, and besides, I couldn't see the red and green port and starboard lights which a ship should be wearing. I switched on my pocket torch (always necessary on a night watch, I had discovered) and had a look at the chart. We were past the Lizard, we thought, and the lights were too high to be buoys. I turned to port to avoid the thing, which seemed to be moving.

The two lights continued to flash, and the whole thing made no sense, so I decided to call the skipper. I didn't feel too badly about waking him up, anyway. I shouted 'Ian!' half-a-dozen times, but got no reply. Finally, I lashed the helm, stuck my head down the companionway and yelled, 'SKIPPER!!!' This message did not reach Ian, but Richard stumbled, shivering, out of his sleeping bag. We regarded the flashing lights together, through the haze. Finally, Richard dug out *Reed's Nautical Almanac*, consulted it briefly, and timed the lights.

'Well,' he said, finally, '*one* of 'em is the Lizard', and went back to bed. I corrected my course quickly, having been steering toward a large and very solid part of Cornwall for the past five minutes. Sure enough, as we drew abeam of the thing, the lighthouse became visible. The second flashing light appeared to be caused by the light striking another, smaller tower of some sort behind the lighthouse. Later, what seemed to be Falmouth appeared and receded.

That afternoon came the highlight of this exciting voyage on the world's fastest one-tonner. We put into Salcombe for more fuel. We had no dinghy and only one jerrycan and the petrol stations were all closed, but the kindly harbourmaster quickly arranged for us to buy ten gallons from the local ferry operator, and we were on our way again faster than if we had had a dinghy and more than one jerrycan and if the stations had been open. Moreover, after crossing the bar at the mouth of the harbour, we found that rare thing, a breeze, and got a couple of hours of sailing in before it died and we had to go back to the engine.

I was on at midnight, then again at nine on Monday morning (the skipper was saving himself again). It was quite foggy, and we were approaching the Needles, the group of rocks at the western end of the Isle of Wight. Ian fiddled with the Radio Direction Finder, did some calculating and said, 'You'll be hearing the Needles fog signal soon.' Soon, indeed, the mournful sound came out of the fog, and shortly afterwards, the proper buoy appeared on the nose. I was impressed.

We were in the Lymington Yacht Marina by eleven, cleaned out the boat, cleared customs, rang Avis for a car and by one I was in bed at the Angel Hotel, dead asleep. It had been the most boring and most exhausting three days I have ever spent on a boat, before or since. So much for exciting delivery trips in fast sailing boats.

The following evening I met for the first time, in person, both Ewan Southby-Tailyour and Shirley Clifford. Ewan (it is pronounced Uwan, I discovered, and Southby, as South) looked more distinguished than his years would suggest, and Shirley looked just like her photograph. Everybody was a bit restrained when we first met at my hotel, two-thirds of the group being British, but after our arrival at a Poole restaurant and the subsequent wine consumed, relaxation prevailed, and I may even have been forward with the lovely proprietress. The evening ended, I think, with an aura of goodwill, in the officer's mess of the Poole Royal Marine Base at three a.m. Shirley reassured me that it would be O.K. with her husband for her to sail with two strange men to a remote island in the North Atlantic. She was a victim, she said, of the 'marry-your-crew-and-give-her-hell' syndrome and could not occupy the same floating object as her husband.

Next day, I visited some chandleries and called in at M. S. Gibb in Warsash and Kemp's in Titchfield. Gibb's make the Hasler Windvane self-steering system, and I met Robert Hughes, their marketing manager and resident self-steering expert, who kindly showed me where and how the things were built. I left almost understanding how the gear worked.

At Kemp's I went over the mast order, and Peter Cartwright and his people made a suggestion or two which seemed useful. Earlier in the day, James Kirkman, sales manager at Brookes & Gatehouse, had spent some time explaining the workings of the instruments I had bought, so my time on the south coast was well spent.

I dashed up to London and spent a day or two taking Ann to the theatre and gaining weight, then flew back to Cork, anxious to see my newly moulded hull and deck.

It hadn't been moulded. Somebody's brother had died, or something, and they promised to have it done and out of the mould on the following Monday, a week later. I was extremely annoyed at the delay, especially since Bill King was coming down for a visit, hoping to see the boat under construction, but I gave the yard my next instalment on the boat, £5,500. It was the largest cheque I had ever written. As long as I was writing big cheques I thought I might as well give John McWilliam some money, and as something extra he threw in a free ride on *Irish Mist II*, which had just been launched.

I leapt at the chance, and soon was crouched on the tiny afterdeck behind the helmsman, getting my first look at what goes on on a big boat. Quite a lot went on, and it would not be long before I got considerably more experience on the big two-tonner.

Bill King arrived on schedule, chugging up to the cottage in a tiny Fiat and we grilled steaks in the backyard, American style, while we talked about boats—his and mine. Bill is a firm believer in Blondie

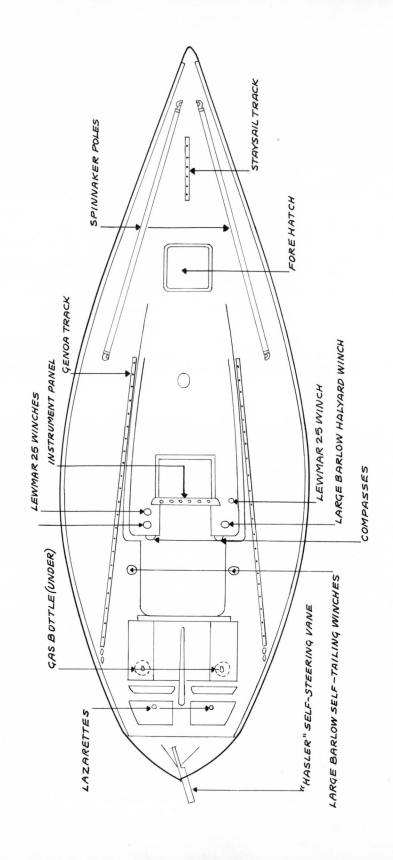

STAYSAIL TRACK

SPINNAKER POLES

FORE HATCH

GENOA TRACK

INSTRUMENT PANEL

LEWMAR 25 WINCHES

LARGE BARLOW HALYARD WINCH

LEWMAR 25 WINCH

COMPASSES

GAS BOTTLE (UNDER)

LAZARETTES

"HASLER" SELF-STEERING VANE

LARGE BARLOW SELF-TAILING WINCHES

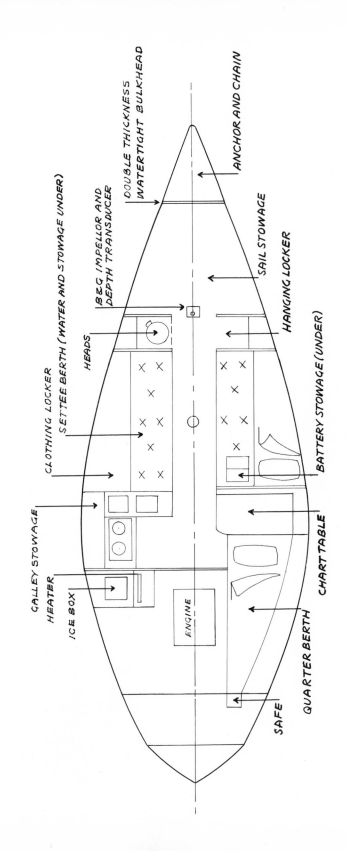

ANCHOR AND CHAIN

DOUBLE THICKNESS WATERTIGHT BULKHEAD

B.&.G. IMPELLOR AND DEPTH TRANSDUCER

SETTEE BERTH (WATER AND STOWAGE UNDER)

CLOTHING LOCKER

HEADS

SAIL STOWAGE

HANGING LOCKER

BATTERY STOWAGE (UNDER)

GALLEY STOWAGE

HEATER

ICE BOX

ENGINE

CHART TABLE

QUARTER BERTH

SAFE

Hasler's Chinese Junk rig, which does have its advantages. It can be reefed in seconds without the skipper's bothering to come on deck, and it is quite possible to cross an ocean in such a boat without so much as donning oilskins.

The following day we went to the yard and Bill saw everything, from the moulding to the joinery. He pronounced himself impressed with the design and spent a long time talking with the various foremen and with George Bush and Barry Burke. We had a good day, and I came away feeling that his trip had been worthwhile, even if we couldn't see my boat. The following day, we went over my charts and made a list of what else was needed for the Azores race. It was startling, the number of charts and publications necessary for such a passage. I had only about half of what was needed.

A local diver came and had a look at my mooring that day, too, replacing some chain and a couple of shackles which had rusted beyond safe limits. I would be ready for the boat long before she would be ready for me.

I spent the weekend in Galway, where Galway Bay Sailing Club was holding its annual boat show. I had worked on the one the year before, and was interested to see how the new edition looked, and surprised to find my old Mirror, *Fred*, on display and for sale. The local doctor to whom I had sold her in the fall had never even sailed her.

By Tuesday, back in Cork, my boat was finally moulded, but not yet out of the mould. I had signed on for a week's cruise on *Creidne*, the Irish Training Ship, the following week, and before I left, Ron and I went down and worked out the deck layout and gave the instructions to the fitting-out foreman. Basically, all the winches and controls were grouped as closely to the cockpit as possible, so that they could be reached and managed by one man. This differed from the standard deck layout, where halyard winches are operated by crew on deck rather than one man in the cockpit (see diagrams). We also had a long talk with the joinery foreman about changes to the interior layout, mostly the addition of extra stowage place wherever possible. That done, I drove to Dublin and joined *Creidne* in Dun Laoghaire.

11 A *Mist* opportunity

Aboard *Creidne*, which is a fifty-foot Bermudan cutter, purchased by the Irish government as a temporary training ship during the planning and building of a new eighty-foot brigantine sail trainer, I was delighted to find Ian Mitchell, an old friend from the Mirror racing circuit. Eric Healy, a toothy, tubby, chatty gentleman with vast experience in sailing vessels all over the world, is *Creidne*'s permanent skipper, and he assigned Ian and me as duty skippers for our planned voyage to Holyhead, across the Irish Sea, in Wales.

First, though, we did a few drills in Dun Laoghaire harbour, picking up moorings under sail, man overboard drills and power handling. Then, up at an early hour for the passage to Holyhead. We had a pleasant and uneventful crossing in lightish winds, and Ian and I both learned the importance of judging tidal streams, for Holyhead turned up on the port instead of the starboard bow, where it should have been.

The trip back on the following evening was more exciting, with the wind blowing Force five and six. Several of our crew had tanked up on beer the night before and, in the short, steep seas we now encountered, they paid the price. Both our watches were shorthanded as a result, and we got little sleep. We underestimated the tide again, and had to put in a half-hour tack to clear the Kish light, just outside Dublin Bay, all the while dodging the Dublin–Liverpool car ferry, which seemed awesomely large from the deck of even a fifty-footer.

Back in Dun Laoghaire we changed crews for the second cruise of the week, only Ian Mitchell and I remaining from the first group. We sailed down to Wicklow, then Arklow, then back to Dun Laoghaire. The week had been especially valuable experience for me, doing everything from foredeck work to cooking to skippering, and giving me experience with the cutter rig, which has two foresails. At Dun Laoghaire, Captain

Healy let me bring *Creidne* alongside under power, which happened without incident, but perhaps a bit slowly. In his evaluation of my week, Captain Healy mentioned that I should be more patient with the crew when skippering, and that I needed more experience under power. I didn't tell him I had never handled a boat under power before.

Archie O'Leary had asked me to come along on the delivery of *Irish Mist* to Lymington the following weekend, and I busied myself with the final details of rounding up equipment for my boat. Manufacturers can be remarkably slow sending equipment, even when it has been paid for in advance, and I was constantly having to chase orders to see that everything arrived in time for the launching.

Quotes for insurance came in, and I chose the one from Hinkson & Company in Dublin, the official insurance agency for the Irish Yachting Association. Their quote was no lower than another company's, but I had been impressed by the personal interest shown. I was paying £200 for coverage in British and Irish waters, singlehanded, and another £150 for the Azores race and the singlehanded return.

One piece of equipment required by the rules of the race was an emergency radio transmitter which would operate on two civil aviation frequencies, to be used in case of losing the boat and taking to the life raft. This signal would be picked up by a commercial airliner, then the rescue services would use the beacon to help locate the raft, which would be very difficult indeed if it had to be located visually. Blondie Hasler, one of the founders of the OSTAR, would probably not approve of this equipment, since he was against any competitor making any use of the rescue services. He has been quoted as saying, a competitor who got into trouble '. . . should have the decency to drown like a gentleman and not bother the rescue people.' I was perfectly happy to have the transmitter aboard.

I was becoming increasingly concerned at the lack of progress on the boat. Barry Burke, who is the second most charming man in Ireland (the most charming man in Ireland, and the nicest, is Dr Eamonn Lydon, of Oranmore, Co. Galway) would, whenever I would come to him, perplexed about the boat's progress, place a fatherly hand on my shoulder and say, 'Now, Stuart, your boat is the most important boat being built in this yard, because of what she has to do, and you just can't rush a boat like that.'

Everything else seemed to be moving along on time, however. One day a few weeks before, the area engineer for Lucas, the electrical equipment people, had turned up at the yard unexpectedly and said he had heard from Hydromarine, the engine people, that I needed a second, larger alternator. He said that Lucas would be happy to provide

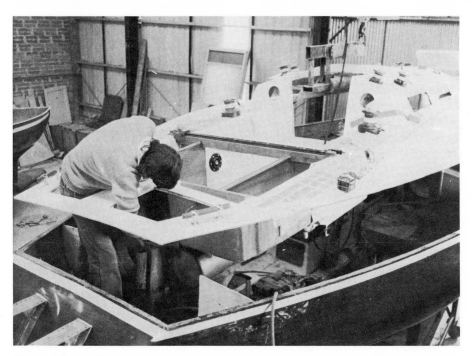

Harp with the lid off.

Bill King checks over a Shamrock in the factory.

it and any technical advice I needed, and now the engine had arrived, the big alternator bolted into place.

Now came the passage to Lymington on *Irish Mist II*, and it proved to be all that the *Golden Apple* delivery had not. We slipped our moorings at Crosshaven in the early evening on Friday May 31st; Archie O'Leary, the owner; Pat Donovan, a Crosshaven publican and regular winch grinder and cook on *Mist*; Peter Walsh, a Cork gynaecologist (just in case); and a student who was studying yacht design in Southampton, and to whom I shall refer as The Kid.

We were soon close reaching in a steady Force six, gusting seven, as darkness closed. In these conditions, watches were being kept in pairs and Archie put me with him, obviously anxious about my lack of experience.

I had made a point, from the beginning, of communicating to the people I sailed with that I was new to larger boats, because I did not want anybody to overestimate my skills, but lately, this was beginning to become a problem. By the time we sailed on *Mist* I had some 1200 miles of offshore experience and had taken an extensive course in coastal navigation, plus about ten days of practical instruction, a week of that on *Creidne*, a larger boat than *Irish Mist*. This was probably more than your average weekend yachtsman would do in two whole seasons, and I could now do, competently, just about anything that needed doing on a boat, barring mechanical and electrical repairs, for which I showed little talent. Certainly, there were things I didn't know how to do on specific boats; I had never worked with slab reefing, for instance, which *Mist* had, but it was simply a matter of becoming familiar with a particular boat's equipment.

I had also discovered two marked advantages which I possessed, both quite accidental and unlearned, but advantages nevertheless. I didn't get seasick, apart from an occasional queasiness, and I was not frightened on boats.

I felt, and still feel, a kind of apprehension before beginning a passage—in the earliest days this had been partly a fear of being seasick, or, perhaps, a fear of being frightened, but I was not subject to the kind of demoralizing, even paralyzing fright that I had sometimes seen in others on a boat. Even now, while we were sailing to windward in the biggest winds and heaviest seas I had yet experienced, I felt nothing but excitement and exhilaration. If Archie hadn't been on deck with me I think I would have been singing or shouting at the top of my lungs into the wind.

Mist bucked into the seas, sending the occasional wave racing down her flush decks to hit us full in the face like a bathtub of water. For some reason, this struck me as funny, and I laughed a lot. I think Archie thought I was hysterical. The two hours of our watch passed very quickly, broken only by the passing of a large, brightly-lit ship, probably the Cork–Swansea car ferry, the *Inisfallen*, which flashed 'K' ('I wish to communicate with you') at us. We had our hands full in this weather, but after looking up what 'K' meant, The Kid answered her, with what signal I'm not sure. I think she just wanted to know if we were all right in the heavy seas, it was nice of her to worry.

Below, *Irish Mist* was, at times, as wet as on deck. The main hatch leaked a lot when a wave raked the decks, pouring water into the lower, leeward bunk, rendering it unusable. There was a spacious galley, but no handholds, these being judged by Ron Holland as weighing too much, and we had a tendency to ricochet about the main cabin when trying to move around. (When Ron Holland dies and goes to Hell, his punishment should be to spend eternity inside one of his own designs with no handholds, sailing to windward in about a Force seven.) If you could stay wedged into a bunk long enough to get the leecloth tied, then you could sleep in reasonable comfort, though. The boat contained the forementioned galley, two lower and two upper berths in the main cabin, a single and a double berth in an after area, and a chart table right aft, where the navigator could, in theory, speak to the helmsman through a small hatch. The rules require certain comforts on a racing yacht, but still it was quite a spartan interior, which Ron thought to be a new high in luxury. (Ron was once quoted by a yachting magazine as saying that all he required for the interior of a racing yacht were facilities for lying down and boiling water. He denies this. I believe the magazine.)

I had a look at the course plotted by The Kid, who was navigating us, and wondered aloud if he were allowing for tidal stream, leeway and surface drift. He saw no point in bothering with these, and as a result, we ended up twenty degrees below our proper course, had to put in an unnecessary tack and sailed fifty miles farther than necessary to reach Hughstown, St Mary's, in the Scilly Isles, our first stop.

I was greatly taken with Hughstown. We were met by the customs/immigration official and advised about anchorages. At one point he asked Archie, 'If you're an Irish ship, why aren't you flying the Irish Ensign?' Archie had a ready and truthful answer.

'My designer thinks flagstaffs weigh too much.'

We visited the local pubs for a few pints and walked through the village, a very pretty one. I resolved to get back here again, maybe singlehanded. That would be a good trial for *Golden Harp*. It was about a twenty-four hour sail from Crosshaven (on the proper course) over open water, without too much shipping about, and it seemed a very pleasant port in which to spend a couple of days.

We had had a bit of excitement coming into the port, when the gearbox seemed not to be working. When we were ready to drop sails the engine started readily, but seemed not to be going into gear. In Hughstown we discovered that the propeller had fallen off, and Archie decided to sail directly on to Lymington without another stop, since getting in and out of ports would be awkward without the engine.

We weighed anchor early the next morning and began a fast passage, reaching and running down the Channel, sometimes flying a spinnaker. By midnight we were past Start Point and headed for Portland Bill and its infamous tidal race. The Kid, for reasons I never understood, had plotted our course *inside* the race, saying something about it being on the rhumb line to the Needles. I had long since given up talking with him about the navigation. The Kid was very good indeed on sailing the boat, nearly as good, I think, as he believed himself to be, but I had grown very weary of the patronizing advice he had been constantly giving, and he and I were not getting along very well.

Now we sailed into Lyme Bay with a following wind of about Force three, on The Kid's course for the inside of the Portland Race. Archie was already worried about going inside and gave Peter Walsh and me explicit instructions not to sail too far out of the bay and, thus, get us into Portland Race. 'Don't get too far in, either,' he had said. 'Gybe if you have to, to maintain your course, but for God's sake *don't* get us out into that race. It's one of the most dangerous places on the south coast of England.'

We sailed on peacefully for a while, and then the wind began to back, and we were having to sail ten degrees above our course to keep from sailing by the lee, that is, with the wind coming from a direction where the boat might accidentally gybe. Soon, we were twenty degrees above our course, and I suggested gybing to Peter. He was doubtful, Archie having given instructions not to sail too far in. Why didn't we sail on the other gybe for half an hour, then gybe back and sail for another half hour, and so on? Peter finally agreed, though reluctantly. We gybed the boat in the gentle breeze, and Archie was on deck like a panther, in his underwear, roaring about 'gybing for the sake of gybing . . .' I think that, under normal circumstances, he would not have reacted quite the same way, but he was clearly anxious about sailing inside the Portland Race, and he would not listen to any explanation of why we had gybed.

Dawn came and Portland Bill was before us. As the wind had backed it had increased sharply, and was now blowing a Force seven, gusting eight. The seas in the race were huge and close together, with waves breaking everywhere. In addition to the normal problems of negotiating the race, we had wind against tide, and a lot of both. Archie was at the helm, and we had to go within fifty yards of the rocks in order to stay out of the race. It was very exciting sailing, with the boat sometimes reaching ten knots when surfing down the big waves, and we made it safely through. Archie, a former international rugby player, admitted having been scared. 'It's like just before playing for Ireland against England,' he said. 'It's running down your legs.'

After the Portland Race, though, Archie would not let me take the helm again, as a kind of punishment, I think, for my sinful gybe of the night before.

The wind now veered, and as we approached the Lymington River, we faced the prospect of beating up the narrow channel against a falling tide and with the car ferry to the Isle of Wight threatening to leave at any moment. We hailed a couple of smaller yachts, asking for a tow, but nobody could hear us, so we started up the river under sail. This involved a lot of very short tacking, and with a group who had never tacked the boat at all.

In her crew cockpit, *Mist* has a grinding pedestal linked to the two huge winches, and Pat took charge of that. Peter and I each tailed a winch, and The Kid stood in the pulpit, yelling, 'TACK!!!' whenever he thought we were getting too close to the edge of the channel. It would be very embarrassing to run the beautiful new yacht aground on a falling tide in one of the most densely boat-populated rivers in England. It went well, though, the boat tacking remarkably quickly and accelerating fast. At times she seemed to be pointing straight into the wind. Finally, approaching the marina, a large yacht gave us a tow for a hundred yards or so, and The Kid cast us off with what he thought was enough way on to drift into a berth. He had misjudged, though, and we began to drift backwards with the tide, with no steerageway. Pat Donovan had the presence of mind to throw a line to somebody on a berthed boat, just as The Kid panicked and threw the anchor out.

We began to clean up the boat and stow the gear, but The Kid, it appeared, was not yet finished with my education. I came very near to throwing him overboard when he began to explain, '. . . how we fold a sail.'

I thanked Archie for the best sail I had ever had. I had been very impressed with the way he had brought us around the Bill in such awful conditions and with his skill in tacking us up the river. I had learned a lot and, surprisingly, was not nearly as tired as after the *Golden Apple* delivery, although the passage in *Mist* had been much more arduous. Now, I left *Irish Mist II*, clambered onto the dock and into the arms of

Ann, who, clever girl, had driven down from London.

We had a pleasant evening in Lymington, and next morning, after running a few local errands, we embarked on the car ferry to the Isle of Wight, which I had never visited. The purpose of the trip was to discuss the rigging of my boat with Ben Bradley of Spencer's, the riggers, but we did some shopping in Cowes' narrow High Street first. It was there I discovered one of the most comfortable of sailing garments, the Javlin Warm Suit, which is a sort of thermal underwear, retaining heat and preventing condensation under oilskins. This would prove to be a valuable purchase.

At Spencer's, Ben Bradley and I agreed on the size and composition of my boat's rigging—Ron had suggested wire rope rather than the standard solid rod rigging, which was fine for offshore racing, but which didn't last as long. We also went a size up on the standard, for extra strength.

Next day, I rang Shirley Clifford in Poole, just to see how she was and to report on the progress of *Golden Harp*, and she reminded me of something I had forgotten. The Azores and Back singlehanded race (AZAB), sponsored by the magazine *Yachting Monthly*, was starting on Saturday from the Royal Cornwall Yacht Club in Falmouth. She and Richard would be there and so would Ewan Southby-Tailyour. Why didn't I come down? Why not indeed? I hired a car, and on Thursday afternoon, took off for the West Country.

I arrived at the Royal Cornwall to find fifty yachts preparing for the next day's start. Almost immediately I bumped into Robert Hughes, the Hasler self-steering expert from Gibb's, who had at his disposal a very fast speedboat, with which he could go from yacht to yacht, offering advice and helping to solve problems. Having never so much as seen a singlehander's boat this was a marvellous opportunity for me, and I made mental notes on layout, control lines, etc.

Richard and Shirley Clifford turned up with their children, and I met Frank Page, the *Observer*'s yachting correspondent, and his lovely wife Sammie; Liz Balcon and Angela Green, also from the *Observer* staff; Angus Primrose, the yacht designer who was sailing one of his own designs, a Moody 33 in the race, and his wife and daughter Murlo and Sally; Andrew Bray of *Yachting Monthly*, who was sailing his Pioneer 10 in the race; and briefly, Claire Francis, the girl who had already done a transatlantic crossing in a Nicholson 32, and now had an Olsen 38 at her disposal, courtesy of her sponsors, Robertson's Jams.

I had dinner with Richard and Shirley, and the following day, Murlo and Sally Primrose and I joined Robert Hughes and his brother, Brian, on whose fast boat we would watch the start of the race. The wind was very light, so there was little drama before the start, but shortly after the start we all became very annoyed with a French spectator boat which was sailing behind Claire Francis flying a spinnaker, thus taking Claire's wind and making it difficult for her to get her own spinnaker to fill. We roared up to the French yacht and, after a few loud words, they bore away and left her alone. It had been a rotten thing to do.

The fleet slowly drifted towards open water, and after a final goodbye to Angus Primrose on *Demon Demo*, we roared across the bay to my favourite village in Cornwall, St Mawes. Then, back to the Royal Cornwall, now strangely empty, and the drive to Fowey, further up the coast, where I was meeting Richard Clifford and Ewan Southby-Tailyour at a Royal Cruising Club rally. I arrived in the pretty village and got a ferry out to Ewan's yacht, *Black Velvet*, only to discover him drinking on another, nearby boat. We passed a pleasant afternoon, and Richard arrived from Falmouth in *Shamaal II*, his Contessa 26, singlehanded. There was then one of the nicest sights I have ever seen on the water. Three of the larger yachts at the rally were tied together in the river, and a very large and exuberant cocktail party took place in the lovely twilight. I added Fowey to my list of harbours to visit.

Richard Clifford invited me for a Sunday morning sail in *Shamaal*, and I accepted with pleasure. We just went out of the river for a bit, then back to a mooring, but it was the first time I had ever sailed on a singlehander's boat, and it was nice to see how expertly Richard handled her. We followed our sail with a lunch of fresh mackerel.

Richard, as I have mentioned, is a Captain in the Royal Marines, and takes great pride in his fitness. He climbs the mast of *Shamaal* without benefit of bosun's chair or steps, just right up it like a monkey. He also takes pride in sailing *Shamaal* without an engine of any kind, and handles her with great flair and confidence.

He gave me something to think about when he said that during the last OSTAR, he had been swept overboard by a wave, saved only by an arm which caught a guardrail. He said that, after struggling back on board, he sat down in the cockpit and wept. I thought, if this hard, tough, superbly fit Marine officer, trained to endure the worst of hardship, had been reduced to that state by exhaustion and terror, what the hell would happen to me under similar circumstances? I could only hope that I would never have to find out.

Back in Cork, the launch was set for June 28th. I wrote out a launch invitation and a press release. I had them both printed and I mailed about fifty invitations to friends and people who had contributed equipment or help on the boat, and I sent press releases to all the Irish newspapers, plus the television service, RTE, along with an invitation, which also invited everybody to a post-launch celebration at the Royal Cork. I also gave invitations to half-a-dozen of the foremen and workmen in the yard who had been particularly helpful, and to the office staff, all of whom had been very nice. Then I placed an invitation in the hands of Pat Hickey, a director of the yard, and handed one to Barry Burke.

12 Launching

Normally I sleep like a stone but for the rest of June prior to the launching, I slept badly. Nor could I read. Even absorbing books like Adlard Coles' *Heavy Weather Sailing* couldn't hold my attention. Every time I read of some heavy weather manoeuvre I began thinking about how *Golden Harp* would react under the circumstances.

But there were bright spots. Vincent Dolan of J. B. Roche, a Cork chandlery, donated a 25-pound CQR anchor and eight fathoms of chain to the project. Alan Best of Croxon & Cobbs, a Dublin chandlery, gave me a trade discount on any gear I wished to purchase from him—they were particularly good on charts—and Western Marine, in Dalkey, gave me a generous discount on the four very expensive Beaufort life jackets I wanted for the boat. Cotter Electronics, a Cork instrument installation company, came and did a first-class job of fitting the Brookes & Gatehouse equipment and the other electrical gear, and gave me a very low price for a great deal of highly skilled work. And George Hayde and his people at Lucas came through on their promise of technical help, doing all the wiring on the batteries and alternators. They also contributed the splitting diodes and isolating switches for the batteries, a generous contribution indeed, coupled with the expensive, marinized alternator.

There were disappointments, too. A Dublin sailmaker who had, three months before, agreed to send a man down to measure the boat for its very important spray hood, now doubled his price in a transparent effort to get out of doing the job. He succeeded. Then a west coast sailmaker agreed to do the job and never showed up for the appointment, after keeping us waiting an entire afternoon. He didn't even bother to phone to say he couldn't make it. John McWilliam, from the heights of the international racing sailmaker, would not stoop to such mundane work either, but at least he had made it clear months before that he wouldn't touch the job with a fork, and he didn't waste my time the way the others had. Before the summer was over, I would suffer from the lack of that spray hood.

I drove up to Tralee and spent an intensive two days with Len Breewood, studying celestial navigation and trying to cram two weekends into one. Len very kindly made me a gift of a light meon anchor which he had made himself. I had been unable to find one like it in Ireland.

Then I drove to Galway and spent an enlightening morning learning how to make a diesel engine behave itself. I had never seen one up close before, but even I understood and came away with a large donation of expensive engine spares. (A few days later, an extremely heavy parcel arrived in the post. Hydromarine had sent me a spare propellor, a very expensive chunk of brass!)

Back in Cork, visible progress was being made on the boat. The keel had been fitted, as had the stainless steel brackets for the self-steering, and I watched as the deck was dropped onto the hull and fastened in place. At last, it looked like a boat!

Acceptances and regrets began to come in for the launching. Sadly, Ann would be working (she designs sets and costumes for films) and could not be in Cork. But other people were coming from all over the country.

At McWilliam Sailmakers, another last minute flap. I had designed a 'Betsy Ross' (the lady who designed and sewed the first American flag) spinnaker, in honour of the 1976 Bicentennial Celebrations in the States, and this called for a circle of thirteen stars on a field of blue. The problem was that John, had, instead of making five-pointed American stars, made six-pointed Israeli stars. Wrong celebration. I had to spend an hour soothing him and telling him how easy it was to make five-pointed stars, and he still charged me three quid apiece for them.

Launch day dawned. Nick and I were at the yard early to find the boat now hauled out onto the quay. The gathering for the launching was scheduled for eight in the evening, and the boat would be open to visitors for an hour before launching at nine, on the high tide.

About eight-thirty, people began to arrive and, suddenly, it all came together. By a quarter-to-nine *Golden Harp* bore every resemblance to a finished boat, her loose wires tucked away and the floorboards and dining table suddenly in place. She was nothing if not a fine actress.

John Smullen, my insurance agent, arrived from Dublin with a lovely young lady and the gift from himself and Alec Hinkson of a handsome visitors book, embossed with the yacht's name. It was a psychic thing,

An hour before the launching.

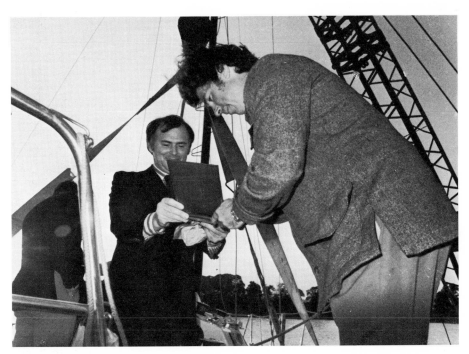

Ron is first to sign *Harp*'s visitors book.

for I had not been able to find one in Cork.

Rapidly, its pages began to fill. Ron Holland and John McWilliam were the first signators; George Kennefick, Admiral, and Raymond Fielding and Harry Deane, respectively Vice-Admiral and Secretary, represented the Royal Cork Yacht Club, now *Harp*'s home club; Ferdia O'Riordan and Michael Healy turned up to represent the Galway club, while Harry McMahon, though we did not know it at the time, was at Dublin Airport, having come from a medical conference in Edinburgh, trying to persuade Hertz to hire him a car without a driver's licence, which he had forgotten; Worth and Pascha Newenham came, so did Len and Margaret Breewood; friends from all over were suddenly there, admiring my boat. Nick had miraculously got the tape player going, and the music added to the festivities. Tom Barker from the *Cork Examiner* was there, and although RTE had had to divert its one Cork camera to a fire, or something, Irish radio was represented in the person of Donna O'Sullivan, a redhead of whom I would see more.

Now all my anger and frustration vanished under a wave of euphoria. It was just as though the boat were actually finished. This moment, which I had dreamed about, but of which I had begun to despair, had finally come. It was all exactly like a real boat launching.

Finally, George mounted the crane, swung the yacht over the quayside, where she paused, her decks level with the stone. Barry Burke, who was not able to be present for the launching, had provided a bottle of champagne, cleverly scored several times so that it would break at the first blow. It is supposed to be terribly bad luck if the bottle doesn't break first time. Laurel Holland, terribly conscious of her responsibility, said, 'I christen this ship "*Golden Harp*". God bless her and all who sail in her', and swung mightily at the bow, missing the boat completely. She hadn't actually touched the boat, though, so no harm done. On her next swing the bottle smashed just the way champagne bottles are supposed to at yacht launchings, and *Golden Harp* dropped into the Douglas River with a fat splash.

It was all so perfect; the water of the river turned to shimmering gold by a huge setting sun, the crowd gathered to wish the boat well, the lovely weather. I made a short speech, thanking Ron and other people who had contributed to the effort thus far, and we adjourned to the Upper Deck of the Royal Cork for a bit of champagne.

Towards the end of the evening George Kennefick made a few kind remarks, and in my response I was able to thank George Bush, whom I had stupidly forgotten to thank at the launching. George had been in charge of the most difficult of all the work, the modifications, and his work would prove to have been done well.

'God bless this ship and all who sail in her!' Laurel Carlin Holland christens
Golden Harp on her second swing.

I hit the bed that night like a felled tree. I don't think I've ever had a
better evening.

The following morning, Nick and I drove to the yard with as much
equipment as we could manage, and we began to load the boat. George
persuaded me to wait for the afternoon tide, to give him time to do a few
more things, and I agreed.

As we were preparing to cast off and the last workman was hastily
gathering his tools to avoid a trip down Cork harbour, I glanced into the
shallow bilges and noticed water there. 'Where did that come from?' I
asked.

'I don't know,' he replied, shaking his head. 'I've mopped her out
every morning since she was launched, and there's still water coming
in.'

Golden Harp, four days after her launching was leaking.

13 The race before the Race

The next three weeks were a whirling potpourri of rage, outrage, relief, elation, depression and exhaustion.

Ron came down to Drake's Pool and shouted from shore that he was leaving for Norway the following morning to compete in the World Three-quarter-ton Championships in his design, the Nicholson 33, *Golden Delicious*. The delays in finishing the boat had robbed me of one of the most important elements of my plan, the presence and advice of Ron, helping me to learn to understand and sail the yacht. Before we sailed for Portsmouth and the MOCRA Azores Race, he would be able to spend only three hours on the boat.

That evening Ron, John McWilliam, Nick and I took *Harp* out into Cork Harbour. Ron did some tuning on the rigging, and John flung up the spinnakers for the people in the clubhouse to see. It was immensely satisfying and a bit unreal finally to see the boat under sail, even if the only headsail we could set was the light genoa, because the headsail reefing system had not yet been rigged. I would not see much of John on the boat, either. His earlier enthusiasm for the project had now been overtaken by a busy sailing season and a full order book for sails.

Harp returned to her mooring in Drake's Pool, where she would spend most of her time until the Azores trip. Killian, George Bush's son, turned up to work on the boat as a freelancer, and things began to pick up. He and Nick began working their way through a list of a hundred jobs. In the rare moments when she was not being worked on, I tried to sail *Harp*. Finally, on a Sunday afternoon, we left Cork Harbour for the first time, even if only for Oysterhaven, a few miles down the coast. I tried my first singlehanded manoeuvres, gybing and tacking. On the way back up the river we stuck on the mud once and had to swing the boom out and heel the boat to get off. The passage to Drake's Pool was a bit dicey at low water. There was a lot of water in the bilges when we got home.

Nick was ill for two or three days, but Killian made progress and occasionally George dropped by with a forgotten bit of gear or to do some small job. He investigated the leaking and said the boat would have to go back to the yard for a haulout to be repaired. It was depressing to contemplate delivering the boat into the hands of the yard again, but there seemed no other way.

Two weeks to go. Bill King and Harry McMahon came down on Saturday night for a day's sail on Sunday. We had dinner at the Royal Cork and met a Dutchman, Eilco Kasemien, who was about to set off for Iceland on his wishbone ketch for his OSTAR qualifying cruise.

The day of Bill's and Harry's arrival had not been without incident. Killian didn't turn up to work on the boat, as it was raining. It was spring tide and there was a southeasterly wind blowing, which pushed *Harp*'s stern in toward shore. As the tide receded, her rudder grounded on the last bit of a shelf which was usually underwater. Nick and I rowed out and got as much weight forward as we could to see if she could be floated off. She was stuck fast. We sat in the pulpit with the liferaft and the anchor for three hours waiting for the tide to turn. The rudder moved freely when she floated, and we breathed a sigh of relief that no apparent damage had been done.

Sunday morning dawned chill and foggy. Bill, Harry and I motored down as far as the yacht club and picked up a mooring to wait for the weather to clear. Later in the afternoon we poked a nose into the harbour to find three hundred yards of visibility and foghorns everywhere. We repaired again to Drake's Pool having never set a sail. Bill felt, though, that he had at least had a good look at the boat and would not feel quite so much a stranger when we left for England. He and his son, Tarka, a Guards officer in London, would arrive on the 23rd to help prepare the boat for sailing on the 25th.

On Monday George came by and we arranged that I would take *Harp* to the yard on the morning tide on Thursday (it is possible to get over a bar to the quay at the yard only two hours before or after high water). Killian did more work one day and didn't show on another. A man came and examined me for my radio-telephone licence and very helpfully searched out some additional information on billing for telephone calls and telegrams via shore stations. On Wednesday a brief letter arrived from Eve Palmer. She and her husband, Alan, had been among my closest friends in London. Alan and I had worked together as co-creative directors at an advertising agency, and had remained close after we had both left the agency. The letter said, 'Dear Stuart, my dear Alan died of a heart attack on Monday, the 7th. Love, Eve.' Alan was a year older than I. I sat in the car in front of the Post Office and reread the letter for half an hour. Its meaning would not change. I would have difficulty thinking about anything else for days.

On Thursday morning Nick and I motored up the river to the boatyard. Hauled out and perched on a cradle *Harp* had that stranded look that all pretty yachts have when they are out of their element.

There was a crack in the epoxy resin which bound the keel to the hull, and daylight could be seen between hull and keel. I left George with a list of jobs to do, told him I had to have the boat back on Saturday and left.

The day got brighter when the book contract and a cheque arrived from my publishers, and Joe McMenamin, who had just bought the Lipton's supermarket chain, promised me some free groceries if an earlier request to the Quinnsworth chain was not favourably received. And a letter had arrived from Quinnsworth saying that they were interested not just in groceries, but in sponsorship! Sponsorship was a constant thorn in my side, what with the recession cutting everybody's advertising and publicity budgets, and this interest helped me to forget for a while the condition of the boat. I rang their offices in Dublin and made an appointment for Monday afternoon to meet with their board of directors to tell them about the project. My mood was further improved by a visit to the yard on Friday, when I found a full crew working away on *Harp*.

At Quinnsworth's I met Don Tidy, managing director, Jim Blanchard, financial director and Des O'Meara, head of their advertising agency. We sat down around a conference table and exchanged pleasantries, then I talked for half-an-hour without taking a breath. I told them about the history of the race and about my boat and my plans. I told them everything I could think of. When I had finished they all asked questions, then Don Tidy excused himself for a few minutes. When he returned he said that, in association with a sister company, Penney's, he thought they would like to sponsor my entry to the tune of £10,000. First, though, he would like me to meet separately with the two advertising agencies involved, explore the opportunities for publicity and have them report back with their opinions. I cancelled my return train reservation and booked on a late night flight back to Cork, then went to Des O'Meara's offices with him. We were unable to reach the Penney's ad man, as he was out of his office at a conference, but Des and I went through the whole project with his public relations manager, and they pronounced themselves satisfied that the opportunity was a good one for Quinnsworth's. They would meet with

Penney's man and describe the project to him. I had to get back to Cork, as we were sailing in four days and there was a lot to be done.

Next day, I plundered the Quinnsworth supermarket at the Douglas Shopping Centre. Don Tidy had rung the manager and told him to give me £200 worth of anything I needed. I had intended to buy our food in England, where it is cheaper, to Shirley Clifford's meal plan, which she had already prepared. Now, in the absence of a meal plan and in the presence of a license to shoplift, I tooled down aisle after aisle of the splendid store, grabbing whatever looked interesting for Shirley (not I) to cook. A couple of hours later I was checking nine shopping baskets past a bemused cashier, the whole thing coming to £199.74. At one point I heard a little girl say to her mother, 'Mummy, that man must have *lots* of children.'

I picked up Bill and Tarka King at the bus station. We spent the rest of the day working on the boat, cleaning her out and fixing as much as we could. By nightfall she was ready to be loaded. We had dinner and went to bed early.

Next morning, Bill and Tarka began loading food and gear. Then Ron came sailing with us in the afternoon for an hour, and in the Force six and seven winds blowing in the harbour we all managed to glean new information from him. We set Fred, as I had begun to call the Hasler self-steering, and he pointed us unerringly at a perch across the harbour, sailing right up to it. Ron pronounced himself impressed.

We spent the remainder of the day packing food into plastic shopping bags and stowing it on the boat. Things were moving well for our planned departure midafternoon the next day, Friday.

As it was, we finished our loading on Friday in time to sail, but we were tired. We had planned to stop and rest for a day in the Scilly Isles, but we hadn't been able to get a large-scale chart of the islands in time, and Bill was worried about going in without it, so we stayed in Drake's Pool for another night, and were invited to Coolmore House for a drink before dinner by Worth and Pascha Newenham.

Pascha and Bill King had known each other since Pascha was a Wren and Bill a submarine commander, both stationed in Ceylon, during World War II. We sat in the handsome drawing room of Coolmore, bathed and shaved, sipping sherry and listening to Bill and Pascha reminisce. The boat was ready. I felt a lovely sense of completion and contentment and expectation.

Next morning, after final stowage and the taking of many photographs, we motored down to the yacht club, had lunch and took on ice, then fuelled and were off. (On the way out of Drake's Pool we had scraped our keel across a mudbank, nearly losing Bill over the pulpit, at the exact moment somebody, probably Theo, had fired a parachute flare from the woods in farewell salute.)

As we motored down the river out of Crosshaven, a single Mirror dinghy followed for a time in our wake. The sight brought back a rush of memories. Roche's Point was soon abeam and, after a lot of sail trimming and adjusting, *Harp* sailed herself for all of the night, as we began to become accustomed to her.

Tuning up.

14 On to Portsmouth

We spent a fine day sailing, fiddling with Fred (who was reluctant to steer on a beam reach), bailing water (which seemed to be coming from forward somewhere, maybe from the long hull fitting) and continuing to build the boat. Tarka finally divulged that he had spent a year as an apprentice with Hickey Boats in Galway when a lad (he had been fired when the foreman found him making a model aeroplane during his teabreak), and he took on the bulk of what had to be done. Bill navigated and I bailed, using the Jabsco electric bilge pump, which had been fitted for just such an occasion. The shape of the hull precluded any more than about two inches of bilges, so two gallons of water could make the interior a miserable place.

We were at Land's End in time to see a beautiful moon rise above Cornwall. By midnight Wolf Rock was abeam, and we altered course for the Lizard, the southernmost tip of Cornwall. As we approached it the tide turned against us, and although we were registering several knots on the speedometer clock, we seemed to be standing virtually still. I spent long periods of my midnight-to-three watch sitting on a cushion on the pulpit, my safety harness clipped to the forestay, watching the moon and the water and the night while Fred steered. It was one of the most beautiful nights I have ever spent on a boat.

By midday Monday we were motoring in a flat calm, and I was using the VHF radio constantly. The Dynafurl had revealed a maddening tendency to separate into two equal halves, and although it could be repaired easily, it was causing us worry; water was entering the boat in increasing quantities, and we were now bailing hourly; and every other fault which had been built into the boat was now surfacing, my own mistakes surfacing, too. During the afternoon a puddle of hydraulic oil collected in the bilges. The trouble was found to be a leaky inspection meter which I should have removed. I sent a telegram to Jeremy Rodgers' Boatyard, the English agents for Stearn, who made the Dynafurl, asking for a replacement to be ordered from the States immediately by telephone. Then I rang Camper & Nicholson's and asked for a haulout and repair of whatever was leaking when we arrived in Gosport. The radio hummed all afternoon with such messages. Bill had flatly refused to sail for the Azores unless we could get the leaking stopped in Gosport. I was in full agreement with him. We motored on.

We also used the radio for social purposes. We made a lunch date later in the week with Angus and Murlo Primrose and, since Ann was in France and would not return in time for our departure for the Azores, I spoke with a young lady whom I had met at another sailing event earlier in the season and invited her down to the south coast for a night later in the week. This young lady shall be known in this tale as The Bird.

By midafternoon on Tuesday the Needles were abeam and we entered the Solent to find it seething with yachting activity. Cowes Week was due to start on Friday, and the narrow body of water was full of boats practising. Spinnakers, tallboys, bloopers and every other sort of sail were everywhere, and it was a very pretty sight indeed. We sailed slowly in light winds past Cowes and past Norris Castle, where Bill's wife, Anita, was staying with friends. Although I had sailed into the Solent before on delivery trips, never had I seen it so dressed with sail. It was very beautiful.

Late in the evening we berthed at Camper & Nicholson's Marina in Gosport. The next day would be Wednesday. The race started on Saturday, and there seemed to be at least two weeks' work to do on the boat. Moreover, we were asking for Campers' help at the worst possible time. The first race of Cowes Week was happening on Friday, and the yard was choked with yachts being readied for the world's premier week of yacht racing. We wolfed down a takeaway Chinese meal and got the last solid sleep we would have for a week.

Early Wednesday morning I waylaid Campers' repairs manager, John Gardner, as he drove through the gate. We went over *Harp* together, and within the hour she was high and dry, sharing Campers' crowded apron with the likes of *Morning Cloud, Golden Apple,* the giant Rothschild yacht and numberless other French yachts, their bottoms being diligently rubbed down by their crews and their skippers complaining loudly (the French are very good at this) to anyone who would listen. A foreman and crew were assigned to *Harp*, and by noon her keel bolts had been loosened to let her dry out in preparation for resealing the keel. Tarka had found a leak in the forward bulkhead and the trouble was quickly located. Every time the yacht hit a wave, water was forced through a gap in the glassfibre seal and into a dead air space under the anchor well, from which it ran through a leak in the 'watertight' bulkhead into the forepeak.

In the afternoon Bill and Tarka left for business in London, to return Friday, and Shirley Clifford rang to say that she would arrive the next day. Robert Hughes from Gibb's turned up and spent four hours tuning and refining the self-steering system and refused to accept a penny. Staggering with fatigue, I took him and his wife out for dinner. I slept on *Harp*, high on the apron, a most peculiar sensation.

I was up at the crack of dawn to let the workmen on the boat and spent most of a frantic day shopping for gear I hadn't been able to find in Ireland. Shirley turned up in the afternoon, and I gave her a list of things to do. The Bird was not far behind. I had not been able to find a decent place to stay in Gosport, and since I had to go to Lymington anyway to exchange a broken meter at Brookes & Gatehouse and collect the new Dynafurl from Jeremy Rodgers, I booked us in at The Angel there. We made a mad dash for Lymington in her car in order to get there before closing time and just made it. Bill Green, Rodgers' man in charge of Dynafurls, broke the news that the replacement hadn't arrived, then gave me tools and instructions on repairing the existing unit. I left instructions to send the replacement on to the Azores so that it would be there when we arrived.

On top of this, The Bird was unhappy. She was unhappy about the sleeping arrangements, unhappy about being in Lymington, and only moderately appeased by a good dinner at Limpets. Next morning she was unhappy about waiting at the post office to see if the replacement Dynafurl would arrive at the last minute, and she pitched a fit when I kept her waiting at a chandlery while I bought other last-minute gear. The drive back to Gosport was completed in stony silence, and our farewell was very abbreviated. That night I noted in my diary, '. . . sometimes I am a very bad judge of women.'

Angus Primrose joined us for lunch at the local pub (Bill and Tarka had returned from London) and gave us a soothing account of his part in the Azores-and-Back Race. The wind, said Angus, had never blown more than twenty-five knots and he had been supremely comfortable throughout. He made a suggestion or two about gear arrangements, and then we were hard at work again. At closing time Camper's put *Harp* back into the water. She looked in very good shape, but we still had ahead of us the job of restowing all her gear and the food. That evening Bill, Shirley and I took the hovercraft to the Isle of Wight for the pre-race party in Bembridge. There were twenty-four hours before the start of the race, and it was the first time the three of us had been together.

Tarka and Anita met us at the party, and we relaxed for a bit and chatted with some of the other competitors. Mike Ellison, of the Amateur Yacht Research Society, was competing in a borrowed trimaran, and I met Bill Howell of *Tahiti Bill*, the Australian dentist, and Brian Cooke of *Triple Arrow*, the sailing bank manager. Both were OSTAR veterans, and I had been looking forward to talking with them about the Race, but with time so short that would have to wait until our arrival in Horta.

Bill returned to Norris Castle with Anita and Tarka, and Shirley and I got the last ferry off the island. When we arrived at the marina we found Richard Clifford asleep on *Harp*'s deck and invited him in. Ominously, Shirley was complaining of not feeling well, but I was too tired to take much notice.

Next morning, she was worse and running a temperature. We put her into a pilot berth and worked around her. Richard tackled a dozen jobs on deck while I emptied the boat of her stores and prepared to restow them. Shirley had pared down our Quinnsworth's groceries to what we would need for the three of us, plus some for my trip back to Ireland. Bill and Anita arrived and Anita sat on the dock, resplendent in a large sun hat, and took notes for a stowage plan as I hustled grub onto the yacht. Bill pronounced himself uneasy about the whole thing. Richard kept looking at the shambles and shaking his head. 'You'll never make it,' he kept saying. Tension mounted. Then the Committee types began coming round and muttering about Shirley's illness. She was refusing to see a doctor, and they didn't like it. I discussed it with Shirley and Bill and proposed a solution. Shirley had been looking forward to the race for weeks, and I was reluctant to disappoint her because of what might only be a twenty-four hour bug.

'Look,' I said to the Committee, 'we'll take her down the Channel with us. She'll probably get better. If she gets worse, there are a dozen places we can quickly put her ashore. If she's not better by Plymouth we'll put her ashore there.' The Committee didn't like it. I pointed out that we weren't violating any race rules. The skipper of a yacht is responsible for deciding who races with him. Bill pointed out that *he* was the skipper and he had agreed to this plan. The Committee said we'd be disqualified if we arrived in Horta without the minimum specified crew of three. They offered us another girl as crew. I pointed out that we would be disqualified if we changed crews within twenty-four hours of the start, and the start was five hours away. They said they'd overlook that. I asked why then wouldn't they overlook the three-crew rule? *Harp* was built as a singlehanded boat; two could handle her easily enough. The rule was obviously aimed at some of the bigger multihulls. They hemmed and hawed. I was beginning to get annoyed. We had much to do and little time to do it. They were wasting what we had left. I finally told them, as politely as I could, that we had made a decision which did not violate the rules and that that was it, so to please go away and let us get on with it. They finally did.

Bill and Richard were still expressing doubts about our being ready for the start, and finally I exploded. 'Look,' I said, 'we have five hours to finish what has to be done. If we don't make it, we won't start, but let's stop wasting time and get on with it. Don't anybody say to me again we won't make it, O.K.?' Everybody went back to work.

The race was to start at seven o'clock in the evening. Incredibly, by five-thirty we were finished. Everything was stowed and Richard had accomplished a lot of absolutely essential work on deck. We had just time to dash for a shower. That finished, we pulled up at the fuel dock just in time to catch the attendant before he left for the day. We took on diesel, then left Richard on the fuel dock. We would not have made it on time without him. We motored out to the line with the main up and immediately found a fouled genoa halyard. I had to go up the mast to clear it but, fortunately, the sheltered waters were flat and motion at the top of the mast was minimal. I took a moment for a look at the view. There were fourteen yachts on the line, only two of them monohulls, *Harp* and *Gypsy Moth V*, being sailed by Giles Chichester, Sir Francis' son. There were a number of large multihulls, in the fifty-foot range, and a number of smaller, cruising types. It was a very pretty sight in the late afternoon sun.

We started badly. The seaward end of the starting line was to be an anchored trimaran, the Committee boat. However, there was also another trimaran anchored nearby, a spectator boat, and we mistook that for the Committee boat. We started third from last. But we had started.

Harp's main saloon from the hatchway, with galley to port and chart table to starboard. Sail stowage in forepeak.

Main hatch viewed from the saloon.

COLOR CODES

GREY - Ground Floor

PINK - First Floor

BLUE - Second Floor

GREEN - Third Floor

BUILDING CODES

0 - Terner Tower

1 - Kimmel Outpatient Surgery

2 - Waters Pavilion

3 - Interfaith Pavilion

4 - Special Care Pavilion

5 - O'Keeffe Pavilion

6 - Franciscan South

7 - Franciscan East

ST. MARY'S HOSPITAL
VISITOR PASS

TERNER TOWER ENTRANCE – GROUND FLOOR

FLOOR	BUILDING	ROOM
		3033

DATE:

MAY 1 2 1995

ADMT 0003b
Rev. 6/94

Harp's gourmet galley. The central heating unit is visible to the lower left of the cooker.

The well-equipped navigation area.

Book Three
15 On our way

As soon as we had altered course down the Solent we found the light wind behind us and got up the Betsy Ross floater. *Harp* began to move. With about five knots of wind showing on the B & G meter, her speed increased from $2\frac{1}{2}$ knots under main and genoa to four knots under spinnaker. We began to overtake multihulls.

Just before Cowes, as we passed Norris Castle, we heard explosions from shore. 'They're saluting us!' Bill shouted. Sure enough, Tarka and Anita were firing the castle's cannon in our honour. As we approached Cowes, the little town's lights began to come on in the dusk. We passed the Italian tall ship, *Amerigo Vespucci*, at anchor, and astern of her, the Royal Yacht. It was too late in the evening for an exchange of salutes, but as we passed, a small, dark-haired woman waved a handkerchief at us from the ship's afterdeck. I think it was the tea lady!

By the time we'd passed Cowes, we had overtaken four catamarans and trimarans and, shortly afterwards, we passed another. Mike Ellison's voice came out of the darkness: 'Your navigation lights are excellent!' He was referring to our very bright Marinaspec masthead light, and it was comforting to know we could be seen from a distance. We were facing heavy traffic in the Channel and God-knew-what in the Atlantic, and I had no wish to experience being run down by shipping. We continued to pull away from Mike's trimaran and, shortly, were hot on the heels of a big cat, both of us doing everything possible to put on speed so as to make the Needles light before the tide turned foul in the Solent and trapped us there in light winds. Then the wind began to freshen and the catamaran pulled slowly away from us, although we could see his lights until after midnight.

We got the featherlight floater down in the freshening winds and continued under the genoa, both of us too exhausted to set the heavier all-round radial spinnaker. Each of us slept soundly when off watch that first night.

We sailed most of the next day with the boomed-out, big genoa, still too tired to get a spinnaker up. The weather was sunny and warm, and we let Fred steer while we lay on the decks and rested. Shirley felt better for a time, then returned to her original condition. She refused all offers of aspirin to lower her temperature, and by late afternoon Bill was saying that we were fast approaching the point where we would have to decide whether to put her ashore in Plymouth. It was not much of a decision. Shirley was only a passenger in her condition, and her condition wasn't improving. We altered course for Plymouth.

Our vague plan had been to sail the boat somewhere pleasant after we'd dropped Shirley, if it came to that, somewhere that I could sail back from singlehanded in order to qualify for the OSTAR. But now I was very dissatisfied with this notion. I put it to Bill that we go on to the Azores. After all, the boat had been repaired, we were thoroughly over-provisioned for the passage, the boat was easily managed by two and our exhaustion was beginning slowly to slip away. Bill readily agreed, to my everlasting relief. I would have been very unhappy if, after all this preparation, we had been forced to change our plans. Now, we began to plan how to lose as little time as possible in Plymouth. Our first plan had been to pick up a mooring in front of the Royal Western Yacht Club or to put into the Mayflower Marina and get a night's rest before continuing. But since deciding to continue to Horta we were in more of a hurry. I got on the VHF and contacted Rame Head coast guard as we approached Plymouth. They said they would arrange for the pilot boat to take Shirley off at the breakwater and would ring Richard to collect her ashore. We pressed on.

Near midnight, as we approached Plymouth breakwater, we were able to contact the Plymouth pilot boat directly on the radio/telephone, and they soon spotted us, sailing slowly under main only, with the decklights on. They came skilfully alongside and took off Shirley, her suitcase and an incredible number of plastic shopping bags. As we prepared to get underway again there was a shout from the pilot boat. Shirley had forgotten a shopping bag. We repeated the performance, tossed the last bag over, then were free. Bill took the first watch and set a course for the point where we had left our original course. Our plan was to return there before continuing to Horta, keeping a record of our lost time in order to appeal to the Committee in Horta to subtract this from our elapsed time. We would also appeal not to be disqualified.

When I came on watch Bill reported that we had been sailing through thunderstorms with gusts up to Force seven and that he had reefed everything and been up the mast twice to retrieve or sort out halyards. I had slept through everything. On my watch little happened except a fishing boat who wouldn't go away, and I spent an hour making sure we didn't hit him or foul his nets. Later in the day I telephoned a Committee member and reported our loss of crew and lodged our request to remain in the race and be credited with the eleven hours it had cost us to put Shirley ashore and return to our original course. He said they would let us know in Horta. I then telephoned my Mother in the United States and Ann, who had returned to London, to let them know of our progress before we were out of range of Land's End Radio. I don't know what the Land's End operators say when they ring a telephone number, but it never fails to astonish anybody who is getting a telephone call from sea. They can never quite believe that it is possible for a small boat out of sight of land to make a telephone call. It is great fun.

It was now Tuesday afternoon, August 5th (we had started at seven p.m. on August 2nd), and the wind was freshening and heading us, an experience which was to be repeated *ad nauseum* for the rest of the passage. We reefed and began to beat. We did not know it at the time, but nearly two weeks later we would be still in identical conditions. At three a.m. the preceding morning I had been wakened by Bill. I was beginning to understand that not only was he a natural pessimist, but that he actually seemed to *enjoy* it when things went wrong. When anybody else would have been depressed and cursing his fate, Bill seemed stimulated.

'What?' I mumbled, rolling over and trying not to let any heat escape from my sleeping bag.

'Bad news,' Bill chirped. I was sure I could see his teeth in the darkness. I was sure he was grinning. The engine battery had shorted and was completely flat. I was sleeping on the hatch to the battery compartment. I struggled out of my sleeping bag and got at the battery. An untaped lead had rubbed against something. I taped it, switched the battery leads to start the engine and began to disappear into the sleeping bag again.

'I've been thinking it over,' Bill said. 'I think we should turn back.' I woke up again.

'What?'

'I'm old and weak,' said Bill. 'You're young and strong, but inexperienced. We've had this battery trouble and the Dynafurl is going to break at any moment. It's your decision, but I just want to put my view to you. If you decide you want to go on to Horta we'll do so.'

I was silent for a moment. 'Old and weak' was not a new theme. Bill

King is a small, but wiry man and he is well-muscled from manual labour on his farm. I suspected that he was stronger than I. In reflective moments he would bemoan his old age, referring to himself as '. . . nearly seventy'. He was not yet sixty-four. Once, over dinner, he'd remarked how well he was feeling, how youthful. I'd pounced: 'But a couple of days ago you were practically on your deathbed.' 'Ah, but now I've had half-a-bottle of wine,' he replied with a grin.

I thought that now I detected a trial balloon of some sort, but I was too sleepy to give him the persuading he seemed to want. 'I'll sleep on it,' I said, 'and we'll talk about it in the morning, O.K.?' I knew that we would cover another fifteen or twenty miles while I slept. The next morning the sun was shining and *Harp* was going well to windward. Bill remarked what a seakindly boat she was. 'She goes to windward so much more comfortably than *Galway Blazer*, with her big spoon bows for running in the southern ocean,' he said admiringly.

'Listen Bill,' I said, 'everything's going well now. The batteries are fully charged, and if the Dynafurl breaks again it's simple to fix with our new tools. We're both feeling better every day. I think we should go on.'

Bill nodded. 'Right. We'll say no more about it.'

We went on.

16 Hard on the wind

A week out. I was sitting in the cockpit in the late evening enjoying the view. There is nothing, absolutely nothing, as beautiful at sea as the sky at night. There seem to be at least four times as many stars as on land, and the Milky Way is just that, a great white swath across a black universe. Then I heard a new noise.

Sailing is not as quiet a pastime as many people seem to believe it to be. Every sailboat is accompanied by a constant little concerto of sounds—water sweeping past the hull, halyards flapping against the mast, the leach of a sail shaking in the wind. A new sound means that something, however small, has changed. The sound I heard now was coming not from the boat, but from the water. I looked over the starboard rail and saw, lit by its phosphorescent progress through the sea, a torpedo coming straight for the boat.

It is amazing how many thoughts and images can pass through the mind in a second or two. I saw the yacht erupt in the explosion, and myself flying through the air, then I thought, nonsense, nobody would torpedo a small boat; anyway, I can see that the torpedo is a living thing. It was a great white shark or killer whale. Bill King had been attacked by one in the southern ocean, now it was happening to us. I saw the boat, holed and sinking, while we scrambled into the vulnerable liferaft and the creature circled the crippled yacht, waiting. Inches from the hull, the great white 'shark' veered sharply away from the boat, as if he had ricocheted. I discovered that I had been holding my breath.

The great white shark/torpedo was a dolphin, the first I had ever seen at night. Now I saw that there was a pair. They did their torpedo act again and again, driving at the yacht, then veering away at the last possible second. Since they provided their own lighting in the phosphorescence, I could clearly see their shapes and features, their smooth grey skins. I sat, transfixed, for nearly half-an-hour as they played their game, having the time of their lives, then they were gone.

We had altered our watchkeeping system now, and we were both well rested. After passing over the continental shelf and leaving the trawler fleets behind, we were in much less danger of collision, being off the most heavily travelled shipping lanes. Now, one of us would stay dressed all night, ready to go on deck if necessary, but not keeping a constant lookout. One night, when I was on watch, I was dozing lightly in my berth, when I became aware that Bill had awakened and was going on deck. I returned to my doze, thinking he had gone up to pee, but suddenly the yacht tacked. A moment later Bill came below again. 'I think I must have developed some sort of ESP in submarines during the war,' he said. 'I just woke up and knew I had to go on deck. We were on a collision course with a very large ship.' I looked out of the hatch and saw the enormous thing about three hundred yards astern by then. I made a mental note always to sail with people who were former submariners, and I wondered if I would ever become that attuned to what was happening around the boat.

We settled into a routine aboard, a routine ruled by the constant strain of being hard on the wind. When a small yacht is beating to windward she will suffer more fore and aft motion and heel more sharply than on any other point of sailing. *Harp*'s motion was very kindly for a yacht of her size, but it is the heeling of the boat which is the most tiring feature of beating. When the boat is heeled at, say, a constant angle of twenty degrees from the vertical, life aboard becomes a continuous struggle with the law of gravity. One is always travelling either uphill or downhill and never on a level path. Ordinary tasks, like eating, become much more entertaining and exciting. I had equipped the galley with some very attractive American dinnerware, each plate of which had a rubber ring around the bottom which, the ad stated, kept the plate from sliding off the table even at a thirty degree angle of heel. The ad was absolutely correct; the plates did adhere at that angle. But what the manufacturers had neglected to point out was that, while the plate would remain firmly in place at a thirty degree angle of heel, the food slides off the plate into your lap. We learned to eat everything from bowls and to hold firmly onto them. They *might* not tip over or slide when heeled, but the suspense was unbearable.

We ate well. In spite of the rigours of beating, I cooked a hot breakfast every morning until the bacon ran out, and we had a hot dinner every night and shared a bottle of wine. Bill, who had a firm rule of no alcohol when singlehanding, relaxed this stance when sailing in company. I think it made us both better company. In the evenings we talked endlessly and listened to tapes from the Monty Python TV series. Bill had never heard of Monty Python, Irish television not having worked up enough courage to broadcast the series to the West of Ireland, and we were both often convulsed. We had a broad range of audio entertainment at our command – the Python tapes, music ranging from Vivaldi to Simon and Garfunkel and, of course, the BBC World Service on shortwave. We even got Radio Two until we were about eight hundred miles out.

We remained fairly busy, apart from sailing the boat. I practised my celestial navigation, comparing my positions with Bill's, and they began to come close. I read a lot, too, getting through Anita's excellent biography of Francis Chichester and a couple of novels. Occasionally, a ship would turn up and we made efforts to communicate. Since the range of our little Seavoice VHF radio/telephone was only about forty miles, we could not communicate directly with land, so I had an idea for sending telegrams via other ships. Merchant shipping did not keep a watch on VHF, using it mostly for port operations, so I kept the signal flags KVHF ready for hoisting. K is the international signal for 'I wish to communicate with you'. VHF, I figured, was self-explanatory.

When we saw our first ship, we got the flags up in a hurry and switched on the radio. Nothing. I lit a white flare. Still nothing. We figured we had not seen him soon enough, and since he was abeam, overtaking us, by the time we got the flags up, he probably hadn't noticed.

Another day, a tiny fishing boat turned up from nowhere. He was apparently a tuna fisherman and the boat was so low in the water that it approached us unnoticed. It had not occurred to us that there would be fishing boats this far from land. He ran alongside us for a few minutes, and in spite of the flags and Bill's efforts in French over the loudhailer (the boat was from a southwest France port) we failed to make him understand that we wanted him to switch on his radio. With lots of friendly waving he disappeared over the horizon.

Our second attempt at a merchant ship bore fruit. We saw it early and had the flags up in plenty of time. I was screeching out 'K' on the hooter as the ship came up to us, and soon I had her radio operator on the VHF. She was an Italian grain carrier, the *Mario Z*, under charter to the Russians to ferry wheat from New Orleans to Leningrad, and she was on her way to the States in ballast. I chatted with the radio operator, a Spaniard, for some time, and he kindly agreed to send telegrams home for us. All merchant mariners, I believe, are bored out of their skulls and perfectly delighted to pass the time of day with a small yacht in the middle of nowhere. It breaks up their day.

Talking with the ship had made our day, too, and there was better to come. For the first time since leaving England, we were freed. The wind backed and we were, at last, reaching. We had two lovely days of it, screaming along in bright sunshiny weather, clocking up our best runs of the passage. Our very best noon-to-noon run was 148 miles. It began to look as if we would make Horta in time for the competitors' dinner on Saturday night, the 16th, and our spirits rose markedly. It had been depressing beating, beating, beating, sometimes laying our course, but even then hard on the wind. This was beautiful sailing, and we began to speculate about what Horta would be like. Bill had sailed past the Azores, but had not stopped there, and I knew only what I had seen in a tourist brochure the Race Committee had sent.

We raised another ship, a German this time, and sent a telegram to Horta giving an ETA of Saturday. Spirits were high.

Then we were headed again. Worse, the wind dropped and we began to experience our first light weather, and from the worst possible place, on the nose. Very depressing. But I was learning an important lesson – that the sea doesn't care when you arrive, or if you arrive at all. The sea is indifferent to the desires of those who sail upon her, and no amount of sulking or swearing will change that. One learns patience at sea, and always the hard way.

Bill got hurt. He had opened a locker under a settee berth and, having forgotten that he had left the lid off, sat down, falling into the locker, the edges striking him around the kidneys. He was obviously in a lot of pain and I was worried. There was nothing in our superduper medical kit, at least, nothing I knew how to use, which would help a ruptured kidney. We were relieved when Bill didn't pass any blood, and we thought that the worst it could be was a bruised kidney. The worst of the pain passed, and although Bill was very sore and uncomfortable, he insisted on doing all the work he usually did, which was plenty. The only concession he made to his injury was to wear a normal safety harness instead of the length of rope he usually wore around his waist.

We plodded on, tacking back and forth to maintain our course, Bill in pain and I irritable, disappointed with our progress. We had hoped to make Horta in twelve days; now two weeks had passed. We worried that *Gypsy Moth* had already left Horta to return to England. We had hoped Bill would be able to return on her, saving the air fare.

Finally, on Sunday morning, we awoke to find Graciosa, the first of the Azorean Archipelago islands, on our route, sitting fat and green in our path. Even more remarkable, we had been freed again and were pointing at the port end of the island, right where we wanted to go, with the wind on our beam. We sailed on towards the island, and as we approached, a small motor launch appeared, towing two large rowboats full of men. Up a stubby mast on the launch, a man was clinging precariously, scanning the horizon. These were the Azorean whale hunters, going after the monster sea mammals as generations of Azoreans have, in an open boat, using a hand-thrown harpoon, their only concession to modernity the little launch which towed them out for their hunt. They gave us a cheerful wave and continued their search.

Then, of course, we were headed again and found ourselves pointing at the wrong end of the island, hard on the wind. Graciosa looked very inviting, with thick, green vegetation, tiny, white villages here and there, and beautiful beaches, with an occasional stretch of dramatic cliffs. We beat our way into the channel between Graciosa and St Jorge, the neighbouring island, and pressed on towards Horta in the shallower, rougher water and freshening winds. We beat all day and all night. I contrived not to wake Bill until he had got some sleep and then turned in at dawn. Sunrise was a relief, for we had been running without lights. About a week out, the Marinaspec masthead light had inexplicably stopped working, and two days before, our spare navigation lights had

Landfall! Graciosa was our first land for two weeks.

gone, too. We then ran with the deck lights on, which took a lot of battery charging, but at least made us visible. Finally, the deck lights went, too, and our last night out we were completely dark and worried about the possibility of colliding with an unlit fishing boat in the blackness.

At half-past-seven Bill woke me. I looked across the water and saw the harbour wall of Horta. We put in a final tack and crossed the finishing line at 08.47, local time. We sailed into the harbour and were directed to a mooring. Somebody on shore set off some fireworks. As we furled the reefing genoa the Dynafurl broke again, but it didn't seem to matter now. We were in Horta. It had taken us $15\frac{1}{2}$ days.

Harp is dwarfed by *Tahiti Bill* in Horta harbour.

17 Horta, sweet Horta

What we saw amazed me. I had been expecting a brown, arid, rather deserted island. Faial was as lush and green as Ireland, and more mountainous. Horta wrapped around the little harbour and ran up the hillside, lots of trees and white buildings.

Gypsy Moth V was moored nearby. Giles Chichester rowed over and invited us aboard for coffee. We began to pump up the dinghy. A motorboat came alongside and deposited a plump fellow in a bright green shirt aboard, waving customs forms. Funny sort of customs man, I thought. He extended a hand and said, in American-accented English, 'Hi, I'm Augie.' And Augie he was. Born of an American mother and an Azorean father, August (pronounced 'Ow-goost') had spent some time in California before returning to live in Horta. Augie was a mine of information and good cheer. Did the laundry need doing? No problem. The electrics need fixing? Can do. I really began to relax. We signed the forms, surrendered our passports to Augie and splashed over to *Gypsy Moth*. There Giles and his crew, Martin Wolford, brought us up to date. *Runnin' Scared* had won the race. We were the last boat to finish, though not last on corrected time (we were also the smallest boat to finish) and three or four boats had retired. Everybody had taken longer than anticipated, so the dinner had been put back to Sunday night. We had missed it by twelve hours. But there was a beach party that night, and probably one every night from now on. The Club Naval, the local yachting, diving, swimming and fishing organiztion, had apparently been given a grant from the government tourist office to entertain the race crews and their wives and girl friends who had met them in Horta, and the Club was having a wonderful time spending it. Nobody's feet had touched ground since reaching Horta. Neither would ours.

We staggered ashore under the weight of an incredible amount of laundry for two people, borrowed the staff shower at the Estelagem de Santa Cruz, a lovely, modern hotel built inside the walls of an old fort next to the Club Naval, then, cleaner and more closely shaven than we would have dreamed possible, tucked into a lunch of *fresh* tuna (I had always thought they were born in cans) fried in batter, local grapes and cheese and a cold bottle of the native white wine, Pico Branco (the local red wine is good, too, if you don't mind your teeth turning blue), all of it a welcome change from the tinned food on the boat.

Thus fortified, we began to lurch about Horta, exploring. We lurched because we had not yet got back our land legs, and the earth seemed to move in the same way as the boat had. We found the Café Sport, which is the headquarters for visiting yachtsmen in Horta. The owner, Peter, receives and forwards mail, changes money, lends his telephone and keeps social intercourse among visiting boats moving at a brisk pace. We renewed acquaintance with other crews over cold beer at the Club Naval and swapped stories about our experiences on the passage out. As it turned out, nearly all the other boats had sailed into a different weather system from the one we had encountered, and while we had had fresh headwinds for virtually the whole passage, they had had free, but light winds and had suffered calms, so everyone had been slow arriving.

I got a list of finishing times, did some calculating and discovered to my astonishment that, allowing for the eleven hours required to put Shirley ashore, we had finished third on handicap, beating *Gypsy Moth* on corrected time. In fact, only *Runnin' Scared* and *Triple Arrow* had beaten us on handicap. But, in spite of our appeal to the Committee, we had been disqualified under the three-man, minimum-crew rule, as had been David Palmer, in *FT*, who had put a crew ashore on another island so that he could make a flight back to England. Our good position on corrected time raised my hopes for the handicap prize in the OSTAR, but much would depend on the kind of handicap I would be assigned for that Race.

In the afternoon I completely succumbed to the lure of being ashore again and moved into the Estelagem de Santa Cruz, revelling once more in clean sheets and hot showers. The boat was a bit of a mess, anyway, since she had begun taking water through the keelbolts again, and everything was very damp. All the rooms had balconies overlooking the harbour, and I could see *Harp* bobbing gently at her moorings, only a couple of hundred yards away. Bill moved into a hotel on top of the hill and got some much-needed rest.

That evening Club Naval threw a beach party for us and, leaning into twenty-knot winds, we ate fish, rubbed with garlic and cooked over a charcoal fire, washed down with Pico Branco. Lots of locals and nearly all of the crews came, and all had a marvellous time.

For the next day or so I wandered around dazed, still unable to believe that I was actually in Horta. Giles Chichester threw a party on *Gypsy Moth* and two other boats were tied alongside to handle the overflow. The conversation and the wine flowed like water, and before we knew it late evening had come and all of Horta's restaurants were closed. Martin Wolford, John Perry, skipper of *Peter, Peter*, who floated about in a white suit, straw hat and ten-day beard in the best beachcomber style and who claimed to be a solicitor in London, and a young lady who had flown out to meet a competitor who had subsequently retired from the race, all came to dinner on *Golden Harp*. We ate and drank well and when, in the wee small hours of the morning, the party began to break up and John and Martin offered to deliver the young lady ashore, I said I would do that myself, since I did not wish to disturb her while she was washing the dishes. I saw John and Martin on deck and to their respective dinghies and then settled down with a brandy while the young lady finished in the galley.

When we came on deck for the trip ashore, *Harp*'s dinghy was gone, in spite of the perfectly good clove hitch I had tied in the painter. It was now two o'clock in the morning, and we were faced with the choice of shouting until we woke some wine-soaked sailor on another boat and asking him to get up, dress and row us ashore in the pouring rain, which had just begun to fall, or staying on the boat. The only sensible thing to do, of course, was to stay on the boat. It was all perfectly innocent, really it was; she stayed in her bunk and I stayed in mine. It is a mark of what dirty minds people have, however, that we took a great deal of raucous abuse the following day.

The dinghy was found, blown ashore at the other end of the harbour. I have never been entirely convinced that John Perry did not have a hand in the undoing of my perfectly good clove hitch. I do not think Martin would have stooped to such an action, but you can never tell about a London solicitor in a white suit and a straw hat.

The days drifted lazily by, with the odd bit of work getting done on *Harp* whenever *mañana* arrived. We continued to be royally entertained by the Club Naval. There was a special dinner at the Café Capitolia for the *last* boats to finish – *Harp* on real time, *Peter, Peter* on corrected time. Augie and Luis, the commodore of the Club, always seemed to be inventing a reason for another special dinner. One day I expressed an interest in seeing some of the island, and a taxi materialized in front of the Estelagem for a free tour. Another time, while I was working on the boat, a motorboat came alongside bearing a bottle of the local brandy – another prize for the last boat to finish. There seemed to be no end to it

The moon rises over the 7,000 ft. volcano on Pico.

all. John Perry threw a party on *Peter, Peter,* a fifty-foot catamaran which could have served as a floating dance hall. Brian Cooke looked around and remarked that there was probably room for a branch office of the National Westminster Bank.

Brian, who had suffered a bad fall from the top of the mast of *Triple Arrow* the season before, admitted that his broken back had not healed completely, but said that he was looking forward to the OSTAR the following season, and to his winter project of attempting to beat Chichester's speed record from West Africa to South America, on which he would qualify his new boat for the OSTAR. There was an impromptu dinner with Mike Best of *Croda Way* and David Palmer of *FT* and his lovely wife, Elizabeth. Mike and David were both, as I was, sailing back from the Azores singlehanded to qualify, and we had an interesting chat about preparing for the Race.

Scrimshaw, etching on whale ivory, is the Azorean art form, and Orthon is its chief practitioner in Horta. Working in a small house crammed to the rafters with whales' teeth and other bones and a great deal of ingenious machinery, most of which he made himself, Orthon, for a modest sum, will engrave the image of a yacht on a polished tooth and mount it. Each competitor was presented with a tooth engraved with the name of his yacht, and these handsome gifts no doubt grace bulkheads in widely scattered places today.

As the week passed, yachts began to sail for England. First to go was *Gypsy Moth*, and she got a send-off of fireworks and hooters. Before leaving for home, Bill Howell laid me out in the cockpit of *Tahiti Bill*, injected me with a pain killer from my medical kit and reglued a loose bridge which had been rattling around the back of my head since Portsmouth. Bill King found a berth with him for the sail back. The other boats followed one by one, until only *Runnin' Scared* and *Harp* were left. I saw a lot of David and Ann Walsh, who were sailing *Runnin' Scared* back, and they planned a trip to Ireland in the autumn, when we would cruise down the south coast. Most days we took *Harp* along the coast from Horta and anchored for a picnic and a swim. In the evenings, Ann formed the diverting habit of suddenly shedding her clothes and dashing into the pool at the hotel on the hill, while the ancient nightwatchman railed at us. I was sad when *Runnin' Scared* sailed out of the harbour and left me to enjoy Horta on my own.

But other boats were arriving all the time, Horta being a prime stop-over for yachts on transatlantic passages : *Charisma* and *Tenacious*, both members of the American Admiral's Cup Team in the recent Cowes Week, came and went; two Canadians sailed in aboard a homemade catamaran; an American couple arrived on a lovely little cutter which sported a square rigged sail; a couple who had briefly been neighbours at Coolmore while building a boat at Crosshaven came in on their way to Brazil; and we all watched with baited breath as the Pilot Boat took a giant, seventy-five-foot ketch in tow just before she drifted onto some rocks, her engine seized and her sails blown out in a gale. She was *Polaris*, a handsome if weathered old boat, built in Germany in 1914, sailed by a very mixed crew which included an English bank manager turned fisherman turned boat bum, a couple of pretty girls and a mad Irish skipper. They were great fun for the rest of my stay and, at last report, Shay, the skipper, and Tim, the fisherman/bank manager, were still in Horta, running a discotheque.

An American ex-marine and now merchant marine radio operator named Bob Lengyl turned up in *Prodigal*, a tiny sloop, and nearly worried himself to death when I told him that the Race Committee was closing the entry list for the OSTAR. He had been preparing for the race for two or three years, but had neglected to reserve a place. He got an application in the mail, pronto.

One of the most interesting people to sail into Horta was Laurie, a wiry Aussie with an impenetrable accent and a wide gap between his teeth. He had a story to tell about that. Leaving Virginia Beach, in the United States, for Horta, he had been caught in a hurricane, then come down with an abscessed tooth. Unable to stand the pain, he had sloshed

David and Ann Walsh aboard *Harp*, anchored off Faial for lunch.

down some whisky, then taken a drill and a self-tapping screw to the roots of the tooth, when it had broken off in attempts to pull it with vice-grip pliers. While he was lying semiconscious in his bunk recovering from that, a supertanker nearly ran him down, scraping his little boat along the entire length of the huge ship's hull and pulling out his mast and most of his stanchions. He had restepped the mast and repaired his rigging at sea, then sailed on to Horta.

Laurie and Len, one of the Canadians, gave me a great deal of help with getting *Harp* ready to sail again, especially with the electrical system, which was performing very poorly. Len had a complete electrical tool kit aboard his boat and worked wonders with a soldering iron.

The people at the Estelagem were interesting, too. A writer and photographer from *National Geographic* turned up, doing a story about the Azores, especially about the whale hunting. Then Perry Mason turned up at the bar one afternoon. Or was it Ironside? Raymond Burr, the actor, for reasons I never quite got straight, owned the lease of the government-built Estelagem. It was very peculiar, at breakfast or dinner, to look up and see Perry Mason/Ironside across the dining room. He gave a reception one evening and is a charming man.

My stay in Horta was stretching pleasantly on, my chief excuse being the non-arrival of the new Dynafurl. There had been some confusion about when and where it was to be sent, and an exchange of telegrams was required before I was notified that it was on its way. Augie and Luis took over from there. They somehow arranged for the pilot of the flight from Lisbon to the Azores to collect the package in Lisbon, then pass it on to the pilot of the inter-island flight, thus saving several days in shipment. Augie then walked me through most of the Azorean Civil Service in order to save me paying exhorbitant duty on the gear, which was being almost immediately re-exported anyway.

A northeasterly gale held up work on the boat for another two days, giving me a breather to enjoy the stories of the anti-communist demonstrations in Ponta Delgado and Horta. At that time Portugal, which owns the Azores, was going through a political upheaval and it looked as though there might be a communist takeover of the country. The Azoreans, who are pro-American, pro-English and anti-communist, did not like the sound of this at all, and a considerable number of them were talking of declaring independence if the communists succeeded in Lisbon. There were very few communists in Horta, but that was apparently too many. There were large demonstrations in the middle of the night, which I slept through. On one occasion the plan had been to burn the local communist headquarters, but it seemed that a rather nice person lived next door and no one wanted to risk the fire spreading there, so a discusssion was held and it was decided to remove the communists' books and papers and burn them outside. The communists retaliated by sabotaging the record player at the local discotheque. On another island a large crowd escorted two communist leaders down to the sea and tossed them in. When they realized that one of the two could not swim they immediately rescued him. The Azoreans are like that.

September had arrived, and I was beginning to worry about getting home before the equinoctial gales started. I had never heard of the equinoctial gales until Bill had casually mentioned their occurrence on the passage out. As I made my final preparations, stocking up on Pico Branco and fresh food from the lovely local market, I checked with the meteorological office at the American air base on another island. There was still a stiff northeasterly wind blowing and I did not relish the thought of beating back to the British Isles after beating all the way out. The duty officer said I could expect the northeasterly to continue for a day or two, then moderate and swing around to the south or southwest. That wind should hold for a few days, then veer to the northwest. He advised me to sail due north until the wind veered so that I would be in a position to take advantage of the northwesterly. He also said that I probably wouldn't experience winds of more than twenty-five knots on the passage home. As it turned out, he was right about everything except that.

On my last night in Horta there was a dinner party aboard *Polaris*, and then I performed the ritual every yachtsman follows before leaving Horta. I painted a golden harp on the harbour wall next to all the other yachts' names and symbols, hundreds of them, including Chichester's, that have accumulated there over the years. The next morning, September 4th, I collected fresh bread and, particularly, banana bread from the Estelagem, gathered my gear together and, with Len, rowed out to *Harp*. Len helped me deflate and stow the dinghy, had a last look at the electrics and got a lift ashore. I started the engine, slipped the mooring and motored past *Polaris* for a last, shouted goodbye. I truly hated to go.

I motored through the harbour entrance, nearly in tears, passing the Pico ferry; everybody aboard waved goodbye. I unreefed the genoa, switched off the engine and started to beat towards Pico in the fresh northeasterly. The 7,000-foot volcano was distinctly outlined against the bright, blue sky, not wearing its usual crown of clouds. It suddenly occurred to me that I had never, not once, sailed *Golden Harp* singlehanded.

I began to consider wintering in Horta.

18 Alone from Horta to Crosshaven

I began to tune the rigging – adjusting the shrouds until the mast was standing straight on both tacks, something somebody had told me how to do in Horta. It worked, and by the time I had finished, my initial nervousness at sailing the boat alone was gone. I began really to enjoy myself; it was a wonderful feeling of self-sufficiency.

Pico began to recede into the distance as we (I always thought of *Harp* and me as 'we') approached Graciosa. As night fell, I navigated from bearings on the many lights dotted about the island. We pointed towards the western end of Graciosa, taking a different route from the passage out, and I rested fitfully, coming up often to check my bearings. I would not really feel comfortable until we had cleared Graciosa and were in the open sea with no rocks to pile up on.

Our first full day out was sunny and clear, lovely sailing, but with the wind still on the nose and dropping. Late in the afternoon I sighted a ship and got my KVHF flags up in a hurry, something I was getting good at. She was the Polish merchant ship, *General Madalinski*, and I got the usual warm reception from the radio operator, who agreed to send telegrams to the States and Ireland for me. The captain gave me a position which closely corresponded with my own navigation, a great relief, since that day I had done my very first noon position on my own. I spent the time reading and listening to the American Forces radio station at Lajes Field in the Azores, which was much like listening to a small-town American radio station. The news was particularly nice to hear, since I hadn't read a newspaper or listened to the radio for more than two weeks.

I got my first good night's sleep and awoke to find us nearly becalmed. I set the drifter and had to work all day at keeping the boat moving in the light airs. At my next noon sight we had only covered thirty-five miles, a

Taking full benefit of the sun. (Why should Rosie Swale sell all the books?)

discouraging figure, but shortly after lunch the wind swung around behind us and I was able to set the Betsy Ross floater spinnaker. The boat's speed increased immediately from two to three-and-a-half knots, more when the wind puffed a bit. Fred steered perfectly, the sun shone, and I had the best sailing I had ever experienced, lying naked on the deck with a glass of wine and soaking up the sun while *Harp* took care of herself. This was a totally sybaritic experience and was the time when I most wished I had someone to share the trip with. Randiness began to set in.

In the afternoon I contacted a Russian merchant ship, the *Alexander* something-or-other, and got the first cool reception in my experience with other ships at sea. They gave me a position and weather report but they didn't seem too happy about it and, since I had sent telegrams the day before, I didn't press them to pass on messages. They divulged that they were en route from Leningrad to Cuba and then signed off.

I went to sleep with the floater still up and woke at midnight to find that the wind had risen and the spinnaker had torn along the starboard leech. When I went to get the sail down, the deck lights shorted again and I had to do it in the dark. I was very sad about the spinnaker, since it had become my favourite sail. It was like seeing a good friend with a broken leg, and I folded it into its bag to await the ministrations of John McWilliam in Crosshaven.

Now I had day after day of free sailing. On the eighth I was making six to seven knots in ten to twelve knots of following wind when a very embarrassing thing happened – or at least, it would have been embarrassing if there had been anybody there to see it. I got a bad spinnaker wrap; my Irish tri-colour all-rounder wrapped around the forestay in the middle, while remaining full of wind at the top and bottom, giving the effect of an over-engineered brassière sticking out in front of the boat. I tried everything I could think of to free the sail, but it refused to unwrap and it began to look as if I would have to climb the mast to unwrap it from the top. It was midafternoon and I decided that since we were still making a good speed I would leave things as they were until it began to get dark. If the spinnaker hadn't unwrapped itself by then, and I fervently hoped it would, then I would go up the mast and free it. In the meantime, a beer seemed a good idea. After all, I was in the middle of the North Atlantic Ocean, and there was nobody there to witness my humiliation. Why not relax?

Five minutes later a Dutch naval vessel, HMS *Zuiderkruis*, turned up and, after making radio contact, the operator's first words were, 'Can we assist you in clearing your spinnaker?' I said I could handle it, and after getting a position and a weather report and ascertaining that they had picked me up on radar at a distance of five miles, I went on deck, shamed into climbing the mast. I waved goodbye to the ship and started up. After ten minutes of swearing and struggling with the bloody thing, it finally came unwrapped, and as the big sail filled I was startled to hear a loud cheer. I swung around to look behind me and found the ship stopped, her entire crew hanging over the rail, applauding. She gave a loud hoot on her horn and was on her way again. So much for privacy in singlehanded sailing.

In the middle of that night I got a fine scare. I was sleeping like a stone when there came a loud thumping on deck. Pirates? I charged up the companionway ladder to find nothing. Then, as I was about to chalk the sound up to a nightmare and go below, the thumping started again. A small, needle-nosed fish had jumped into the cockpit and was thrashing about the floor. I caught him and returned him to the sea. I don't know if I really rescued him, for at that moment a pair of dolphins appeared and started into the phosphorescent torpedo act again, and he could have made a midnight snack for one of them. I watched, still fascinated, until they departed, then crawled back into my bunk.

I settled into a deep contentment. I was comfortable, well-fed and doing what I had been planning for months. The nearest problem was eight hundred or so miles away, and I was enjoying my solitude and self-sufficiency. The only fly in the soup was that *Harp* had never stopped taking water, and as time wore on she took more and more. There was so much that it was impossible to isolate and tell where it was coming from.

nuts /

The electric bilge pump had packed up again and, since the intake for the main pump was too large to collect water in the shallow bilges unless the boat had three or four inches of water inside her, the only way to bail was with a sponge and a bucket, and it wasn't much fun. By now I was taking out about twelve gallons of water four times a day, and anything that touched the floor got soaked immediately.

I continued north, and the barometer began to drop. When it went down six millibars in four hours I knew I was in for a blow, and I reefed before dark even though the wind had not yet risen; I had no wish to have to reef in the middle of the night with the deck lights not working. By morning we were in our first full gale ever. Fortunately, the wind was still behind us and we were able to maintain our course while running before it with a double-reefed main and the genoa reefed to storm jib size. We were making excellent time.

I settled into a heavy weather routine. This consisted mostly of staying in my bunk, sleeping or reading, apart from a periodic look around the horizon for shipping and a check of the sails and decks to make sure nothing was chafing or coming adrift. And bailing. As the weather deteriorated, the leaking got worse. I began to become accustomed to living in my sea boots, with two inches of water slopping about the cabin. There were two exterior forces as well which made things less comfortable. One was the mini-broaches. When a boat 'broaches to' when running before the wind, she suddenly veers and tries to point into the wind, ending up beam-on to the seas and the wind. This can be very dangerous, and *Harp* never quite performed the manoeuvre. What she did do was begin to broach, then correct. Fred, like any self-steering gear, could not anticipate the action of a following wave the way a helmsman can. He could not correct the boat's direction to allow for a wave which was about to change it. Rather, he would have to wait until he felt the yacht beginning to change direction, then correct. This resulted in a sort of 'mini-broach', in which the yacht would start to veer abeam to the wind, then resume her proper course. The effect on the occupant of the boat and the contents was much like that on the occupants of a car which, travelling at, say, forty miles an hour, suddenly and sharply swerves to avoid another car backing out of a driveway, then continues down the street. If I were standing, cooking for instance, when the mini-broach occurred to port, I would be tossed across the cabin to land on (or under) the chart table. This is not as much fun as it sounds.

The gale moderated after half a day, but we were left with a large, old sea running. Still, we had about twenty-four hours of relative quiet, with winds of no more than about twenty-five knots, and this seemed something of a rest. The most tiring part was the constant bailing.

Then the barometer, after rising a bit, began to fall again. In the first gale it had bottomed at about 1,014 millibars. It was there again when I went to bed on the night after the gale. During the night I dreamed, first, that I was being tossed around in a rubber dinghy. I think this came from being bounced in my bunk between the foam rubber cushions of the settee-back on one side and the lee cloth on the other. Towards morning I began to dream that I was lying on a beach with the sea lapping against the sand a few inches away. When I woke there was, instead, about four inches of water lapping around the inside of the cabin. Thinking for a couple of minutes that the boat was sinking, I began bailing. There is a saying that there is no more effective bilge pump than a frightened man with a bucket. This, I can say from personal experience, is true. Finally, when I had scooped up as much water as possible with the bucket and had to resort once again to the sponge, I realized that the boat was not sinking, that she had merely begun to take more water. During the next three days she took more than three hundred gallons.

When I had recovered enough from my fright to look around me, I found that the barometer had plunged to 1,008 during the night and that there was forty knots of wind blowing outside. While bailing, I had hardly noticed the motion of the boat. Now I did. I could hardly fail to notice it because suddenly the boat committed one of her finest mini-broaches; I was lifted off my feet, flung across the cabin from the chart table and deposited squarely on top of the cooker. By the time I had disentangled myself from the stainless steel fiddles on top there was the distinct smell of gas in the cabin. I quickly got into the cockpit locker and turned off the gas supply at the bottle. From that time, when I wanted to cook, I had to go into the cockpit, turn on the bottle, then dash into the cabin and light the cooker before enough gas collected to cause an explosion. Once the flame was burning it seemed to consume any excess gas from leaks, but I used the cooker as little as possible from then on. What really cut back my use of the cooker was the fire.

I had gone through my cockpit/cabin drill, but the disposable cigarette lighter was damp and slow to light. When I finally got a spark and a flame the whole cooker, both burners and the grill, burst into massive flame. My reaction still astonishes me. There was a fire blanket near my right hand and a fire extinguisher at my left knee; either would have quickly extinguished the fire. But instead of using one of these I simply *blew*. The fire went out like the last candle on a birthday cake. I was very, very careful with the cooker after that.

Now, with so much wind blowing, the sea around me became an even

Force 10 in the Atlantic. The waves never look as large in the photographs.

more fascinating place. It wasn't very cold and rain was spasmodic, so I would sit in the watch seat in the companionway and watch the gale. Fortunately, the wind had risen slowly and without changing direction radically, so the seas, though large, were regular and from the same direction. Using the mast as a guide, I reckoned the waves were a bit over twenty feet in height, and I watched transfixed as *Harp* rose to meet each one. Just when it seemed that a giant sea would overtake us and fall on top of the boat, the yacht would rise to meet it, and the wave would pass harmlessly under us. As the wind rose even more there seemed to be waves breaking everywhere, but never one immediately behind us. When that happens, when a yacht is 'pooped', an incredible weight of water falls onto the boat, serious damage can be done and gear washed away. If the main hatch has been left open the cabin can fill with water and the boat founder.

Harp surfed down the big waves, often exceeding her theoretical hull speed of about eight knots. I have one vivid memory of sitting in the watch seat, watching the instrument dials; the yacht suddenly accelerated to 9½ knots, surfing down a wave, and the windspeed indicator was registering a steady forty-five knots with the wind dead astern. This meant a true wind speed of fifty-five knots, or more than sixty miles an hour. The noise and spray were incredible, but knowing that I had a good boat under me, it was not frightening but exhilarating.

Now my spare navigation lights failed. On reaching Horta I had found that the masthead light had simply disappeared, blown away on the passage out. Now, with the spares gone, too, I was reduced to one small, battery-operated, white light, which I taped to a stantion so that it could be seen all round. In a lull, when I started to unreef the genoa a bit, the Dynafurl parted again, the top half of the top swivel staying up the mast with the halyard and the bottom half sliding down the twinstay with the sail. As long as the wind was behind us this did not pose much of a problem, since we could still sail very fast under the double-reefed main only, so I lashed the sail to the deck along with the number one genoa and sailed on. I would have to climb the mast and retrieve the top half of the swivel before I could set a headsail again. Quite apart from the weakness in the Dynafurl, which would have to be redesigned, this meant that there was a gap in my sail plan. The smallest sail I had aboard was the number two reefing genoa, which meant that if the Dynafurl failed in heavy weather I needed a smaller sail to set until I could repair it. I would have a lot of rethinking to do when I reached Ireland, but then, that was what the qualifying cruise was for – to expose weaknesses in the boat and her systems. On that basis my cruise from the Azores was already an outstanding success.

The storm continued for nearly three days, with the wind only occasionally dropping to gale force. My reaction to being tossed about was, surprisingly, not fear, but anger. I found it difficult to sleep, because when the boat mini-broached and woke me up my anger at being awakened made it difficult for me to go back to sleep. This cut into my reserves of strength, and the constant bailing kept me tired, but I became really exhausted only once.

At dusk on the 13th, I went into the cockpit to change the battery for the navigation light and discovered to my horror that both the number one and two genoas were dragging in the water, attached to the boat only by a shackle at their tacks. If I lost those sails, or even if they were badly torn, I would have no headsail to set and would be at the mercy of the wind, unable to sail in any direction but downwind. I was afraid to stop the boat and let her lie ahull, abeam to the seas, so I left her on her course, got into a safety harness, clipped onto a jackstay and crawled forward to the foredeck, where I could reach the overboard sails.

With the additional drag from the two big sails, the boat had slowed to about four knots and was heeled more sharply. Large amounts of seawater were washing over me, and when I began to try to pull the sails aboard I discovered that they seemed hopelessly entangled in the lines, now broken, which had been laced through the guardrails to keep the sails on deck. Also the drag on the sails was incredible. It was like trying to haul in nets full of fish, singlehanded.

As if all that weren't enough, I began to hallucinate. I had read about the hallucinations of singlehanded sailors. Joshua Slocum believed he had been assisted by a Portuguese seaman from another era, who appeared when he needed help. Others have written of shouts from on deck when something had gone wrong. Still others have seen and talked with friends or relatives. My hallucination was somewhat more mundane. The telephone rang.

Of course, there was no telephone on *Golden Harp*, but that did not stop it from ringing. What's more, it was a *French* telephone, like the instrument in a cheap Paris hotel room. It rang and rang. It was a bit like being in the bath, hearing the phone ring and being unable to answer it. My thought process went: dammit, there's the phone, must answer it; no, can't answer it, got to get these sails aboard again; wait a minute, stupid, there *is no* telephone; . . . there's the phone, must answer it. . . . It went on and on as I struggled with the sails, the same thought pattern turning over and over in my head; I could no more stop it than I could stop the phone ringing.

It took me more than an hour to haul the sails aboard again and secure them, the whole of the time being drenched, often with my feet dragging in the water as I tried to find a position where I could get a better grip and more purchase on the dragging canvas. Twice I almost lost a seaboot, rescuing it just as it was being washed from my foot. Finally, I had both sails aboard on the foredeck, lying spreadeagled on top of them to keep them from going again. Foot by foot I slid their bulk back towards the cockpit, taking infinite pains to see that no part of them slipped overboard again, because now they were attached to nothing except me. I made the cockpit, pushed the sails in ahead of me, then collapsed on top of them. At last, I thought, I can answer the telephone. It stopped ringing, just as it always does when you've struggled out of the bath and, clutching a towel about you, raced through the house, leaving a trail of wet footprints. Later, when I told a friend about this, she said, 'Suppose it *hadn't* stopped ringing?' That is a terrifying thought.

I lay in the cockpit for half-an-hour, not even budging when another squall hit. After all, *Harp* was steering herself, and I couldn't get any wetter. I think that if anything else had gone wrong at that moment I would have been unable to do anything about it. It is that degree of helpless exhaustion which is so dangerous to the singlehander. Sometimes, if you can't cope you can't live. It's as simple as that.

Soon after this delightful evening the storm began to abate and the wind veer. By morning the wind was ahead of the beam, still blowing about thirty knots. We were close reaching under double-reefed main only and our speed was down to two knots. Without a headsail we were going to make little progress, and if the wind continued to veer we would end up pointing at France instead of Ireland. There was nothing to do but go up the mast, retrieve the halyard, fix the Dynafurl and get a headsail up. I made my first attempt almost immediately; I got about two steps up the mast, a forty-knot squall hit and I was quickly down and into the cabin again, very chastened.

Next day, Sunday, I tried again. The wind had dropped further, but there was still a big sea running and, the wind having veered, it was now coming from two directions. I got as far as the crosstrees this time before I chickened out and retreated to wait for the seas to go down. Finally, late Monday afternoon, I made one last assault on the mast. I ran the boat off to steady her as much as possible, got into a harness and started laboriously up the stick, clipping one of the two stainless steel carbine hooks onto a higher step before unclipping the lower one. That way if I slipped I would always be hooked onto something, although I didn't relish the thought of swinging around like a pendulum from a rope clipped to a mast step. I stopped at the crosstrees to rest my hands, which were already very tired from gripping the steps so tightly, then continued. Step, hook to next step, unhook from lower step, step again. It went that way for all of the mast's thirty-eight foot height, until finally, I was clinging desperately to the top, both arms wrapped in a bear hug around the mast. It was necessary to hold on very tightly still, for the boat was rolling in the confused seas, and the mast was cutting an arc of fifteen to twenty feet at the top. Had I lost my grip there would have been a kind of slingshot effect, and I would have been catapulted off the mast into the sea. I stuck an arm through a mast step so that I would have a free hand, praying that the boat would not do a snap roll and break it at the shoulder, and started to haul down on the halyard.

The whole of the time I was at the top of the mast I thought about two things to the exclusion of everything else. The first was Brian Cooke falling onto the decks of *Triple Arrow* and breaking his back; the second was a teenager jumping from the yardarm of a tall training ship that summer, striking the water and dying instantly from the impact. That was all I could think about.

When I had finally inched my way back down the mast I sat on the deck for fifteen minutes until I could make a fist again, then repaired the Dynafurl and hoisted a foresail. I was nearly as tired as I had been after rescuing the sails. And while I had been doing that, other things had been going wrong. I discovered that when falling off a wave, *Harp* had jammed the log impellor up into the hull, freezing the mileage recorder. This was easily put right, but I had no idea when it had happened, and not knowing what distance I had covered screwed up my dead reckoning mightily. I hadn't had a firm position fix for several days, because there had been so little sun, and with my dead reckoning out, I was very unsure of my position and still not close enough to land to use radio direction finding.

Then the engine refused to switch off. I had been charging batteries, and the lever which controlled the accelerator had jammed, corroded by seawater which had reached the engine through the cockpit floor, which was almost impossible to seal properly because of the way it was constructed. No amount of easing oil or blows with spanners and winch handles would free the lever, so now the only way to stop the engine was to turn off the fuel cocks and let it run out of fuel. Then, before starting again, the fuel system had to be bled to get out the air bubbles in the fuel lines.

Next, my last disposable lighter refused to work and, having no matches on board, I had no way to light the cooker. This meant no hot food, no hot coffee, no hot anything, and I was not looking forward to eating cold tinned food.

Finally, the main alternator failed, but at least I was able to plug in the spare. It would only charge one battery at a time, though, so I had to switch leads to charge both batteries, and I could not run the engine and use the other electrics at the same time. Bloody nuisance it turned out to be, too.

By Tuesday I was over the continental shelf and had a rough RDF position, but I was anxious to contact a ship for a tighter fix. Once, when I had been lying on the foredeck repairing the wiring to the forward navigation light, I saw first one, then four ships, but the engine was running at the time to charge batteries, and I couldn't use the VHF. In the early hours of Tuesday morning I spotted a brightly lit fishing boat nearby and began signalling KVHF. He apparently didn't read morse, so he came over for a closer look. He was soon well within shouting distance, but my electric loudhailer chose this moment to malfunction, so I was reduced to shouting 'VHF – Radio' as he circled and came up about fifteen yards off my starboard quarter, running alongside and slightly behind us. It was a huge, steel trawler, a hundred feet or so in length, and she was wearing a German or Dutch name which I could never quite read. I shouted repeatedly, but there was lots of shrugging and shaking of heads by everybody on deck.

Suddenly, the helmsman put his helm over all the way to port – I could see him in the wheelhouse spinning the wheel – and started across my stern without reducing speed in the least. I froze in the cockpit as the enormous trawler came towards us – I was actually looking *up* at her bows – and waited for the crash. The thought raced through my mind that if I went below to get a lifejacket I would be trapped there when the collision occurred, and that there was no time to launch the liferaft. So I stood, clutching a winch and bracing myself for the blow. He missed *Harp*'s stern by less than ten feet, and took more than ten years off my life. I turned the signalling torch on myself and waved him away. I resolved never again to ask a fisherman for help or advice unless I was really in a bad way.

I got little sleep that night, keeping a watch for shipping, then at dawn I saw a strange shape sticking up over the horizon. My binoculars had fogged up from being wet, so I couldn't identify it, but I thought it must be an uncharted oil rig, and since it seemed to be receding I went below to make a cup of coffee. I had begun hearing jets passing overhead now and figured I must be on the London–Cork air route. A few minutes later I heard a helicopter, a very loud helicopter, and went on deck to find a US Navy chopper hovering about a hundred feet directly above the boat. I looked astern and there was the largest warship in the world, the U.S.S. *Nemitz*, a nuclear-powered aircraft carrier over a thousand feet long and with a crew of five thousand. I knew about her from an interview I had heard on the BBC with one of her officers. She had been on a courtesy visit to England and she was now apparently trying to find out what the hell a small yacht was doing sailing about with no one at the helm. I waved at the chopper crew and they went away, apparently satisfied that there was someone on board. Again, the engine was running and I couldn't call her up on VHF.

Tuesday passed quietly with light weather and occasional rain, but towards evening the wind freshened and I was running at a good clip, on course for Crosshaven, I hoped. I was still a bit shaky on my position, getting good bearings from Old Head of Kinsale and Galley Head, but unreliable ones from Round Island, in the Scillies. I began to plan a landfall about eight-thirty the following morning at Robert's Head, just outside Cork Harbour.

I stayed up all night, waiting for Old Head light to appear, hoping it would be in the right place. To make matters worse, my log had begun to overread, destroying my dead reckoning. It began to drizzle heavily and I worried about visibility as I approached the Irish coast. About four a.m. I sighted the loom of Old Head light. I got a quick bearing on it and settled down for the light itself to appear. Roches Point light at the entrance to Cork Harbour would appear, eventually, too.

Then the visibility closed in completely. The drizzle obliterated everything, and although I kept a vigil I was never able to raise either light. Dawn came in the most peculiar way. It was not possible even to tell where the sun was rising. Everything just changed from black to ever lightening shades of grey until it was full daylight. All I could see was fog. There was not even a bird about to give me some idea of how far I could see. The terrible thing about fog is that it makes it impossible to judge distance.

I sat in the watch seat with the depth sounder in my hands watching the water get shallower and shallower. I expected an eight-thirty landfall and the soundings seemed to confirm this. I felt pretty sure that I would sight land somewhere between Kinsale and Cork, a distance of about fourteen miles, but then I could also make my landfall east of Cork. I could only point the boat at where I thought Robert's Head might be and hope for the best.

The sounder read forty fathoms, then twenty, then fifteen, then twelve. Eight-thirty came and went. Still no land. Still no visibility. Then I heard a noise like the engines of a ship. Oh God, I thought, as if making a landfall in no visibility weren't enough, I've got to dodge a ship or fishing boat. I doubled my efforts to see through the fog. All I could see was a white line on the water just ahead of us. A streak of detergent foam washed out of some river, I thought. Then, less than two hundred yards dead ahead, a large, green cliff appeared out of the fog. The noise had been the sea pounding against it. The white line had been the surf. I had found Ireland; now I had to find Crosshaven.

I gybed very quickly indeed and sailed east along the coast, keeping it barely in sight. Since I wasn't certain where I was, I didn't want to run onto rocks on one part of the coast, thinking I was on another part. The visibility cleared slightly and I saw a buoy, Daunt Rock buoy. After a week without a firm fix and in two hundred yards of visibility, I had found Robert's Head on the nose, and twelve minutes late. I was giddy with excitement.

I contacted Cork Harbour radio and asked them to have customs meet me at the Royal Cork and to ring Nick at the cottage and ask him to help me get into Drake's Pool and pick up *Harp*'s mooring. I sailed along into the entrance to Cork Harbour, still in poor visibility, and picked up Ringabella Bay and Ringabella House on its shore. The hammer-headed water tower on the hill appeared. It was not until I was abeam of Roches Point that the fog lifted enough for me to see the lighthouse.

As I began to tidy up the yacht and get ready to take the sails down I looked up to see a Mirror dinghy sailing past me out of the harbour. Her skipper was singlehanded. I thought, where the hell is he going, singlehanded on a day like this? And then, I wonder if he knows what he may be getting himself into?

I motored up the river into Crosshaven and picked up a mooring in front of the Royal Cork Yacht Club. The place was deserted, apart from a steward and the customs men, who were there to meet me. As the customs men were going ashore, Nick appeared, roaring down the river in his rubber dinghy, standing up and waving both hands. He came aboard and we motored up to Drake's Pool and picked up *Harp*'s mooring. Fred greeted us in a frenzy as we stepped ashore in front of the cottage, and I wondered, how many people can sail 1300 miles and never touch land until their front doorstep? I turned and looked at the yacht swinging peacefully at her moorings.

Golden Harp was home.

Fog begins to lift at the entrance to Cork harbour.

19 Back home

Everything seemed very peculiar at home in Ireland. I had the usual problem of stopping the earth from swaying, of course, and the rooms of Drake's Pool Cottage seemed vast after the confines of *Harp*'s cabin, which had seemed so roomy at sea. I staggered about the cottage, babbling incessantly to Nick and Heather. I could *not* stop talking. We had dinner at a local restaurant. The thing I had missed *second* most on the passage was food cooked by somebody else, served on a white tablecloth, with cloth napkins. I talked all through dinner and straight through till bedtime. By the time I crawled between my first clean sheets and soft bed in thirteen days I was hoarse from talking.

The autumn was a busy time, and the boat was my first priority. The broken log was returned to Brookes & Gatehouse for servicing; Hydromarine sent a man down to recondition the engine; Lucas replaced both alternators and the splitting diode, all of which had been corroded into uselessness by seawater entering the engine bay through the cockpit floor; Derek Holland, a neighbour at Coolmore and a former ship's engineer, rewired the whole boat; Nick fitted my ingenious little heater; and the cooker, which hadn't liked it when I had been thrown on top of it, was replaced. I raced the boat in a Sunday event in the harbour, crewed by a tribe of local Lydens, and she took twenty gallons of water in three hours, so Harold Cudmore and I packed the keelbolts with lifecaulk and hemp and retightened them, and this greatly reduced the water she was taking, though it did not cure the condition.

John McWilliam and I flew to the Southampton Boat Show and I got a lot done there: Marinaspec kindly replaced the blown-away masthead light, explaining that there had been a faulty weld on a few lamps and they had not been able to track me down; I met Jim Nolan of Barlow Winches, who agreed to loan me a pair of big self-tailing winches and a larger halyard winch; and I had a talk with Camper & Nicholson about bringing *Harp* to England for repairs. On the flight back we had to divert to Shannon, as Cork Airport was closing, and the following morning we had a beautiful, low-level flight over the green Irish countryside, stopping at two small airfields along the way, one of them the front lawn of Kilbritain Castle, near Kinsale.

Before leaving Horta I had asked Luis, Commodore of the Club Naval, to write to the Royal Western, confirming that I had left Horta alone; on arriving in Crosshaven, Harry Dean, Secretary of the Royal Cork had also written to them, confirming my singlehanded arrival. I had then, as the rules required, submitted a list of my noon positions between Horta and Crosshaven, and on September 29th I received a letter from Lloyd Foster saying that I had been accepted for the Race pending only the final inspection of *Golden Harp* in Plymouth the week before the Race. This was a monumental landmark for me. I felt that I had now accomplished a great part of what I had set out to do: I had learned to sail, got experience on a wide range of boats, completed one navigation course and half of another, making up in practical experience what I had lost in classroom instruction; I had planned and had the yacht built, equipped her, sailed her 1400 miles with Bill King and 1300 singlehanded; I had experienced an enormous variety of conditions, and both the boat and I had stood up to them. All that was left to do before the Race was to overhaul the boat completely and make the refinements I had already worked out in my head.

The autumn slipped by in the most pleasant sort of way. David and Ann Walsh from *Runnin' Scared* came over for a weekend sail to Kinsale, followed closely by Ann, who came for several days.

Harold Cudmore, Ann and I sailed down the south coast of Ireland, stopping for the night and a good dinner in Kinsale, then proceeding to the lovely little village of Castletownsend, where we were joined by Philip McCauliffe for a short passage on to Baltimore. We ate well, slept well and spent many pleasant hours in the West Cork pubs. After a day in Baltimore the weather went to hell and showed no signs of clearing up, so we got a lift back to Cork and left *Harp* on a mooring there for collection later.

While awaiting *Harp*'s return, Ron Holland, John McWilliam and I appeared on the Irish version of the TV quiz show, To Tell The Truth, in Dublin. We all claimed to be me, and a panel had to figure out who was lying. We must have been pretty good liars, because only one of the four panellists guessed correctly. Highlight of the programme came when a panellist asked Ron what a centreboard was. 'Something that keeps a boat from sailing sideways,' Ron answered. The panellist turned to McWilliam. 'And what do you have if you don't have a centreboard?' she asked, pouncing on him for an answer. 'A boat that sails sideways,' replied John. We had a great time.

I had hoped that the television appearance might help pave the way towards finding a sponsor for the Race, something that had eluded me so far. (There had been a regretful letter from Quinnsworth on my return from Horta, saying that they had decided they could not participate.) But the recession of 1974–75 had hit Irish businesses hard and advertising budgets, never very big in Ireland, were at an all-time low.

Ron, his design business expanding rapidly, bought a farmhouse across the river from the Royal Cork, made plans to renovate a pigsty and turn it into a design office and hired an assistant. O. H. Rogers, a young man from Florida, had been Ron's first client when he struck out on his own, the resulting boat being called *Cherry Bomb*. Now, after campaigning for a couple of seasons, O.H. was apprenticing himself to Ron, and he would turn out to be a big help to me in preparing *Harp* for the Race.

On November 20th, O.H. and I motored *Harp* up the harbour and delivered her into the hands of Southcoast Boatyard for her 'immediate' repairs. On December 1st I left for my home in Georgia, to spend the Christmas holidays there. I stopped by the yard to see how work was progressing. I had a talk with them about it, and they promised to be well along with her when I returned in January.

I spent five weeks in the United States, working on the early chapters of this book, visiting friends at home in Manchester and in Atlanta, looking into the family business, a clothing business rapidly becoming a department store which needed further expanding, and just relaxing. Only one event occurred that might have had a bearing on my entry in the OSTAR.

My last week at home I did something to my back which made it very sore – a muscle strain, I figured. Then, on the day of my departure for Ireland, then London and the Boat Show, I was bending over the sink shaving when something down low snapped, and I was suddenly in excruciating pain. I tried to delay my departure for a day, but the only flight I could get was the one I was already booked on so, walking in a rather peculiar way, I arrived at Atlanta Airport, struggled up to the Delta Airlines ticket counter and said in a strangled voice, 'Do you think you could get me a wheelchair, please?' The startled girl behind the counter picked up a telephone, spoke a few words and within seconds a man with a wheelchair materialized at my elbow. My ticket was processed instantly, the gross overweight of my luggage was overlooked and it was shipped straight through to Shannon Airport against all regulations, since I was stopping in New York.

Moments later, I was being wheeled at a rapid clip down the $2\frac{1}{2}$ miles of corridor to my departure gate (it is *always* $2\frac{1}{2}$ miles to my departure gate), sailing through the security search with hardly a pause, the wind made by our swift pace cooling our passage every step of the way. It occurred to me that I had inadvertently discovered a wonderful new way to travel in airports. I recommend it.

I was put on the plane before the other passengers, made comfortable, given a quick glass of water with which to down the large pain-killing pill I was waving about and given the first drink when the bar opened. At Kennedy Airport, New York, I was met by another wheelchair, my New York-routed luggage appeared in record time and I was deposited in a taxi without my feet ever touching the ground. I believe I was passed from person to person so quickly because each of them was afraid I would die while in *his* hands.

After a two-day visit with my old friend Carol Nelson (remember our experience with the Mini and the incoming tide?), this entire performance was repeated in the Aer Lingus terminal at Kennedy, at Shannon Airport in Ireland and, eventually, at Heathrow in London. This, I thought, is the only way to go.

I hobbled through the London Boat Show, stoned out of my mind on painkillers (all the back doctors in London had flu or were out to lunch, or something – it was a week before I could persuade one to see me), tying up loose ends as best I could. I ordered an excellent new suit of oilskins from Morgan of Cowes, the yachting tailors, and four Javlin Warm Suits, in case I decided to take the northern route in the OSTAR. I also bought an excellent signalling torch, and Camper's measured the standard *Golden Shamrock* at the show in order to make a much-needed sprayhood for *Harp*. I also had a long lunch with Tim Stearn of Stearn Sailing Systems to talk over modifications to the Dynafurl, and he promised to supply me with a newly designed unit which would solve all my problems.

When I finally got to see a back specialist, he ushered me into a large, gilt office, poked here and lifted there, ignoring my screams, then laid me on an altar-like slab in the middle of the room, stuck a needle into my backbone and lubricated my spine as if it were the crankshaft of a Fiat 128. This hurt only slightly more than my original back problem. I left his office, poorer by £25, clutching an orthopaedic back cushion and a prescription for more pain killers.

Fortunately, my back did not hurt when I lay down, which meant I could sleep well, or when I was sitting, which meant I could eat well. Ann and I toured our favourite restaurants, and I enjoyed the occasional dinner with other old friends. Angela Green of *The Observer*, whom I had met at the start of the Azores-and-Back Race in Falmouth the summer before, joined me for lunch one day and brought me up to date on the Race. At the close of entries on December 31st, 1975, there had been *197 entries received*, and all hell was breaking loose in the yachting press. Disaster at the start was being predicted from all sides, and there was a lot of bitching about the acceptance of Alain Colas' huge, 236-foot yacht, *Club Méditerranée*.

I, for one, was delighted to have the big boat in the Race, since it stimulated so much discussion, although I was not going to be sailing across her bows at the start screaming 'Starboard'.

20 Reconnoitre

In early March I made a reconnaisance trip to Plymouth and managed to combine business with pleasure. I had never been to Plymouth and I was anxious to have an advance look at the facilities well ahead of the race. Ann joined me for the trip. First, we visited the Royal Western Yacht Club of England, which would be organizing and running the Race, and as we walked down the steps to the waterside setting of this famous club, we were greeted with a bit of drama.

A bright red trimaran was in a lot of trouble. He had apparently tried to sail away from a club mooring, had got into irons and drifted dangerously close to the rocky shoreline and to the sea wall in front of the club. He had flung out an anchor, which was holding his bows off, then somebody from the club had thrown him a stern line. That somebody turned out to be Lloyd Foster, Secretary of the Royal Western and every OSTAR aspirant's main contact with the Race Committee. Lloyd turned out to be a calm, boyish-looking fellow, in spite of long naval service going back to navigator's duties on a World War II destroyer. He settled Ann in the drawing room with a magazine and sat me down in his office. I had a dozen questions and he had all the answers: yes, there was a good yard where I could make advance arrangements for any last-minute repairs to *Harp*; yes, there would be a shipping company at Millbay Docks to collect any extra gear from competitors and send it ahead to Newport; no, we could not use our engines at the start, no matter how many boats entered; yes, there would be plenty of space for 197 boats in Millbay Docks, etc., etc., etc.

We chatted for an hour or so, and I was relieved to discover that the Committee was unperturbed by all the criticism being levelled at the Race. The controversy centred around the number of boats and the fact that a singlehander cannot keep a lookout at all times which, according to the Race's detractors, made singlehanding unseamanlike. What the detractors preferred to overlook was the fact that the start would be postponed if there were fog or extreme weather, and that every entrant knew that he would have to stay awake for the first two days of the Race until he was across the continental shelf and out of the fishing fleets.

The editorials and letters to the editors seemed to imply that the full burden of avoiding collisions rested on the singlehander, and that merchant ships and fishermen were never at fault in these circumstances. On the passage from Horta to Crosshaven I had once, on a bright sunny day, come on deck to find a large, merchant vessel dead ahead of me on a reciprocal course. I had borne away to avoid a collision, and as the big ship sailed past me I never saw a soul on her decks or bridge. This is not an unusual situation at sea, and I believe that if the standard of watch maintained on most yachts, even singlehanders, were maintained by merchant seamen and fishermen, there would be few, if any, collisions at sea.

Lloyd seemed to feel that no matter what the Committee decided, they would be criticized, so they would simply press on, organizing the Race the way they felt it should be done.

We left the Royal Western and had a look at the place where all the OSTAR yachts would congregate in late May. Millbay Docks is a large, concrete tidal basin with locks which open an hour before every high tide and close an hour afterwards. It is surrounded by businesses and warehouses, most of which have something to do with shipping or ships, and, apart from its size, is not a very impressive place. It is doubtful if the place has ever been drained and cleaned, and there is a story that once, when someone fell into the water, he was, after having his stomach pumped out, detained for forty-eight hours in hospital for observation. I do not doubt it.

We drove over to the Mayflower Marina and were given a tour of the facilities there, and I booked *Harp* in for the week prior to the deadline for being in Millbay Docks. Finally, we visited Alec Blagdon's boatyard, and I made arrangements for a haulout in case it was necessary before the race. Alec Blagdon is a kindly man with a West Country accent, and we shared mutual friends in Cork. I felt he would be very helpful if I should need it.

I had hoped to take Ann sailing, but on our return to Cork found that the yard still had not finished with *Harp*. A couple of young American students turned up, sent along by Bill King, and I put them to work rubbing and antifouling the yacht's hull. Eventually, we got her in the water. At last she seemed right. I was certain that a lot of detail would still need work, but she was basically watertight and sound. Her keel had been removed, a reinforced glassfibre 'shoe' inserted between the keel and the hull and the keelbolts glassed in. This stopped the movement of the keel which had loosened the bolts and allowed water to come into the boat. The Brookes & Gatehouse log hull fitting had been replaced, the first one having been incorrectly installed; lockers had had floors glassed into them to keep bilge water from entering; the port pilot berth had been enclosed to make a clothing locker – now the heater radiator would warm two dry lockers as well as the boat; a beam had been glassed under the deck to reinforce the inner forestay deck fitting; a padeye had been fitted to the foredeck and bolted to a bulkhead – I could now set a small storm jib flying without taking down the headsail, just roller-reefing it; the interior of the cabin had been relined with foam-backed vinyl; the windows had been removed, resealed and bolted on; a new Sestrel Porthole compass had been fitted, which could be read both from the cockpit and from the cabin; all the deck blocks had been removed, resealed and refitted; the decks had been given a new and better non-slip finish; and a dozen other small refinements had been made.

She was mine again. *Mine.* I had six weeks to get her ready for a May 15th departure for Plymouth. Harry MacMahon and I would take a leisurely week to sail her there, the last unhurried time I would have aboard her. I looked forward to it eagerly.

21 A last Irish Spring and final preparations

That there was much more work to be done on the boat became clear the first time I sailed her. Some friends and I set off for a weekend cruise to Kinsale, and as we were sailing out of Cork Harbour one of the girls asked for a sponge and bucket to do some bailing. Thinking that a little water had been left in the bilges I handed down the bucket, but a couple of minutes later, as *Harp* heeled in a gust, there came a shout from below that water was pouring into the boat. I jumped down the companionway ladder to find a heavy stream of water entering the cabin from the engine bay. I got the ladder and engine bulkhead off and found a bare-ended hose pouring water into the boat at the rate of about twenty gallons a minute. Fortunately, a wine cork was the perfect size to plug the hose, and with a jubilee clip tightened around the whole thing, it seemed watertight. But we cancelled the cruise to Kinsale and settled for a sail around Cork Harbour, uncertain what other defects we might find.

Harold Cudmore and I planned to sail up to Galway, to arrive in time for the West of Ireland Boat and Leisure Show, now a fixture of the Galway Bay Sailing Club. O.H. and I sailed the boat as far as Kinsale, from where Harold and I would depart for the long cruise down the southwest coast, then around the corner and up the west coast to Galway, but we began to get bad weather forecasts for the west coast and I decided to drive. We left the boat on a mooring at Kinsale, for collection later. A couple of days afterwards I was awakened at eight in the morning by the ringing of the telephone. (After six months of clawing my way through the Irish Civil Service, I had finally got a phone by appealing to a politician friend, who wrote one letter and did the trick.) A voice asked if I were the owner of *Golden Harp*. I was. She had broken her mooring and was aground on the opposite bank of the river.

I dressed and made the fourteen miles to Kinsale in record time, my heart in my mouth and pictures running through my mind of *Harp* lying on her topsides, her mast tangled in some tree. I arrived to find that Courtney Good, a Kinsale businessman and owner of another *Shamrock*, had pulled her off with the club crashboat, and we got her onto another mooring quickly, completely undamaged. It had been the scare of my life, for if she had been damaged badly I would have had one hell of a time getting her right again in time for the Race. I sailed her back alone in a Force seven, but it being an offshore breeze the sea was flat. It was only the second time I had sailed her singlehanded, and it was very exhilarating.

I drove up to Galway for the Boat Show, which was bigger and better than ever, and for a last goodbye to the people who had given me my first opportunity to sail, both in dinghies and cruising boats. At the dinner, I was allowed to say a few words, and I presented a cup to the club to be given each year for the best cruise by a member. I was very sad to think that I might not see Galway or any of my friends there for a very long time.

Some time in April I read that there was a second Irish entry in the OSTAR, Patrick O'Donovan, and that he had just sailed into Kinsale at the completion of his qualifying cruise in a thirty-one-foot trimaran. The next day I was invited to dinner at the O'Donovan's Cork home, where Patrick and I got acquainted and compared notes on our preparations. He mentioned a new marine radar detector which would sound an alarm in the presence of radar signals from another ship, and this sounded a good idea, since the OSTAR rules prohibited radar on the yachts participating. I ordered one immediately.

Patrick had had his problems with getting a boat ready and would have more. He had planned to sail *Lillian*, a fifty-five-foot proa, in the Race, and had actually qualified in her, but on a return trip from Ireland to England with *Lillian*'s owner, the proa had capsized in a Force ten and Patrick and the owner had spent eighteen hours in the liferaft, tied between the proa's floats, until they were picked up by a fishing vessel. When they returned to look for *Lillian* she could not be found, and they learned subsequently that she had been taken as salvage by a Russian ship, sawn into manageable pieces and left on a quayside in Cairo, of all places. All Patrick had got back was his passport, forwarded by the British Consulate there. Now he had bought my friend David Walsh's trimaran, *Silmaril*, and qualified her. The following morning he stopped by Drake's Pool for a look at *Harp* and more conversation. Patrick, who was only twenty-three, would be one of the youngest competitors in the Race. Born in Cork, he was now living in England and was preparing his boat there.

Ron and Laurel Holland moved into their new home, Strand Farmhouse, in Currabinny, across the river from Crosshaven, and for the first time Ron had a proper design office. From his drawing board he had a view of the Royal Cork and the members' yachts moored in the river; he could see all who came and went. Shortly before I left for Plymouth, he and Laurel cruised down to Kinsale with me, the first time they had sailed together in two years, kept apart on the water by Ron's increasingly busy schedule and Laurel's pregnancy. Kelly, the Holland daughter, was a big tot by now, and Laurel was pregnant again.

Now I applied to the Irish Yachting Association to be examined for the Yachtmaster's Certificate, the culmination of a programme I had been working on for more than a year. To my astonishment and consternation, I was told that I did not have enough experience to sit for the examination. The Yachtmaster's programme called for forty-eight hours of classroom instruction (I had had sixty-four); six days of practical instruction (I had had ten); and five hundred miles of offshore cruising (I had submitted a logbook documenting more than four thousand miles offshore, 1300 of it singlehanded). I was incensed to be told that I did not have enough experience even to *take* the examination. If I took it and failed, fine, but I did not feel I should be denied the examination after so much work. Apparently, the difficulty had stemmed from a report about my training cruise aboard *Creidne*, when Captain Eric Healy, the skipper, had suggested I needed more experience of handling the boat under power, and that I had been impatient with the crew when skippering. I agreed that these had been justifiable, constructive criticisms at the time, but since then I had sailed more than three thousand miles and amassed a great deal more experience, and I did not feel that comments made a year before still were applicable. At the suggestion of a friend, I wrote to the president of the IYA, explaining my position and requesting an examination before I left for Plymouth. I waited nervously for a reply.

My back problem had begun to abate now, after more than three months of pain whenever I stood up or walked for more than two or three minutes at a time. The lower back pain had extended to the sciatic nerve, which runs from the hip down to the foot, then given way to severe muscle cramps which continued for some weeks. I had been to two more back specialists; one had given me muscle relaxant injections which helped somewhat; the other had told me just to wait and it would go away, and he prescribed a very embarrassing, steel-braced corset to be taken on the transatlantic crossing in case the fractured disc slipped out of place again. Having always been extremely healthy and unaccustomed to severe pain, I lived in terror of the thing recurring in mid-Atlantic. My last treatment came from a quack, an Irish farmer who seemed to be able to 'divine' and treat the source of pain, much in the way that some people are able to divine water. His treatment had the most immediate and dramatic effect of all, although it did not cure the problem entirely, and I was unable to see him again, as he lived some distance from Cork. So I tucked my corset into a locker on the boat and hoped for the best. I was also very careful about lifting things and favoured the injury whenever I could.

At the Easter bank holiday weekend I planned a return to the Scillies with some friends, having been very impressed with the islands when we stopped there during the *Irish Mist* delivery trip the spring before. We spent a delightful, sunny weekend, listening to the local male choir in the pub and seeing Harold Wilson, recently retired as Prime Minister, strolling on the beach with the giant Labrador which had once nearly drowned him when the dog had capsized the dinghy from which Mr Wilson was fishing.

Our passage back was pleasant and fast, taking only twenty-seven hours in a good breeze. We had been supremely comfortable on the boat, what with the central heating and the stereo, and after much work the bugs were finally being ironed out. *Harp* was beginning to be something like ready for the Transatlantic. No serious water was coming into the boat, although there were one or two minor leaks I hadn't yet located; the new Dynafurl supplied by Tim Stearn was working well in its newly engineered form; and with the addition of the new storm jib, which could also be used as a reaching staysail, the sail plan now seemed ideal.

Back in Cork my sextant, which had been left with Henry Browne & Son for reconditioning and correction, arrived, not having withstood very well the tender mercies of the British and Irish postal systems, and I packed it back to London with Harold Cudmore, who was setting off for America and Spain on the international yacht racing circuit.

Word came that I would be examined for the Yachtmaster's Certificate after all, and a Mr O'Gallagher met me at a Cork hotel, examined me closely for more than an hour and pronounced me passed, to my intense relief. I believe I was the first person to be certified under the programme.

I made a final dash to London where I conferred with my publishers and took care of last-minute details. Ann and I continued our restaurant research, and I had another lunch with Angela Green of the *Observer*, when I learned that Chay Blyth, who had damaged his huge trimaran, *Great Britain III*, in a collision with a ship, would not be participating in the Race. All doubts about the entry of Alain Colas had been resolved, though, and he would be sailing his 236-foot *Club Méditerranée*. Colas had nearly severed his right foot when it was caught in an anchor chain the year before, but he had made a remarkable recovery and, wearing a special boot, had made his qualifying cruise in the Mediterranean with a crew of *forty*. He would do another 1500-mile singlehanded qualifying cruise prior to the Race.

Henry Browne & Son, when they saw the state of my old sextant, promptly gave me a new one without charge. *That* is the sort of customer relations that maintains an outstanding reputation, as was also my experience with the Omega Watch Company. I had purchased an expensive Omega wristwatch which had performed erratically; when I got no satisfaction by reporting this to the American importers, I wrote directly to the company in Switzerland, and within a very short time, the Irish distributors had replaced the old watch with a brand new Omega Seamaster electric wrist chronometer, which performed beautifully. In general, I found that most of the suppliers I dealt with took great pride in their products and were always ready to make adjustments when warranted. Only two or three times in the eighteen months that I dealt with manufacturers was I disappointed by a supplier's attitude. During the whole of the project I was badly let down by only one equipment manufacturer.

My final task in London was to buy provisions for the Race, and for this I went to Harrod's, that superb department store in Knightsbridge. On the Azores trip I had become bored very quickly with my diet, and I was determined to take more time and plan my menus more carefully for the much longer transatlantic passage. I chose Harrod's because their magnificent food halls are stocked with a huge variety of *main courses* in tins. Any supermarket has a lot of canned food, but the choice of main dishes is poor. Harrod's has everything, from the simple to the exotic, and I filled four or five large shopping carts with stews, chicken, sauces, cheese, meats and, best of all, American snack foods I had grown up with, packed in tins to preserve their freshness. It was expensive, but I would eat very well indeed.

Back in Cork I had less than a week to dismantle my life in Ireland and prepare for a new one at sea. Those last days were wildly busy, every moment taken up with packing, paying bills, making arrangements to have mail forwarded and goods shipped to the States. I was very sad at the thought of leaving Drake's Pool Cottage, and even sadder to leave Fred, but he had, fortunately, practically adopted the McCarthy family, who lived near the main gate of Coolmore, staying there whenever I left Cork for a few days. They loved him and he loved them. It is not every dog who has the opportunity to choose his own family.

Harry was arriving on Friday and we were sailing for Plymouth on Saturday. On Thursday night Ron and Laurel Holland arranged a farewell dinner at their new home in Currabinny; John and Diana McWilliam were there; Nick, Theo and Heather came; so did Derek and Carol Holland and O. H. Rogers – all of whom had done so much work on the boat that I could never thank them sufficiently. Friends Donna O'Sullivan and Carey O'Mahoney came, too, and we had a good dinner and a fine evening, even if it was tinged with sadness for me.

On Friday the removals people came and took away the personal belongings I would be sending to the States, and in the afternoon Harry McMahon arrived. We worked the rest of the day getting gear sorted, had a farewell drink at the Royal Cork Yacht Club, a steak at the Overdraught, and got a good night's sleep. Next morning I took Fred's bed, bowl and rubber mouse to the McCarthys' and made my farewells there.

We loaded all the gear onto the boat and began stowing everything, tied up next to Nick's boat in Drake's Pool. Fred had been behaving oddly for the last twenty-four hours; I think he knew something unusual was up. The day before he had turned up in Carrigaline, apparently looking for me, something he would not ordinarily do. Now, after my choked-up goodbye, he sat on the stone slip in Drake's Pool and solemnly watched us working on the boat. I had explained to him long before that he would never be allowed on *Harp* until he had learned to use a marine toilet, and after a few instances when he swam in circles around the boat, demanding loudly to be hauled aboard, he had given up, and whenever I rowed out to the boat he habitually departed in a huff for the McCarthys'. He sat there the whole morning watching. Finally, we had the last bit of gear stowed, we had made our last goodbyes to Nick and we were ready to leave Drake's Pool for the last time.

We started the engine, cast off Nick's lines and, as we motored around the first bend and out of Drake's Pool, the last thing I saw was Fred, sitting in front of the cottage, watching.

22 Cork to Plymouth

An hour later we were in a full gale. The southwesterly six-to-seven wind that had been forecast had become southerly and Force eight. Harry, who does not have the world's best sea-legs the first day of a cruise, was very ill, and in his bunk. I reefed us down to storm canvas, set Fred (the Hasler Vane Steering), and relaxed as best I could in the seas. The gale continued all that day and all night, and morning brought little relief and bad visibility. Our first intended stop had been the Scilly Isles, but I had borne away onto a close reach to ease our motion and keep up our speed, and we made our landfall at Land's End early the following evening. Faced with a hard slog to the Scillies, I decided to turn left and reach to St Ives, on the north coast of Cornwall, instead. It turned out to be a delightful alternative.

Not having a large-scale chart of that part of the coast, I telephoned the St Ives Harbourmaster on the VHF and got excellent approach instructions, and we were anchored in the lovely bay by midnight, ready for a much-needed night's rest. There was no customs officer in St Ives, but we went ashore anyway the next day, saw the town, had dinner and returned to the quay to find two police detectives waiting for us at the dinghy. Our identification and explanations were accepted, but it was clear that, the political situation being what it was, the constabulary was taking a close interest in any visiting yacht flying an Irish ensign.

After another night in St Ives, we beat our way around Land's End in a Force seven wind, Harry now fully recovered, and made our way in moderating weather to St Mawes, my favourite Cornish village, just across from Falmouth. I had radioed ahead to arrange for the customs launch to meet us there, and on arriving we did a little square dance with them in St Mawes Harbour as they came alongside us, bending a stanchion or two and the top shaft of the self-steering, but finally we were safely moored.

Two days later we sailed to the entrance of the Helford River, and as we started to motor up that beautiful Cornish estuary, the engine, though it continued to run smoothly, ceased to drive the boat and we had to be towed to a mooring.

The following morning Harry went over the side in a wet-suit to see if the propellor turned when I put the engine in gear. It did not, but we didn't know if the propellor was freewheeling on the shaft, or if the hydraulic drive wasn't turning the shaft. The best solution, after several calls to Hydromarine in Galway, seemed to be to continue to Plymouth without the engine and there look for repairs, so we slipped our mooring and sailed to Fowey, enjoying a light-weather spinnaker run along the way. We were able to sail up the river into Fowey and anchor without incident, had dinner ashore and a drink at the Royal Fowey Yacht Club and another on a Royal Navy training yacht anchored alongside us, then sailed for Plymouth the next morning.

It was a beat in fresh winds all the way, but finally we were sailing past Plymouth Breakwater, past the Royal Western, around Drake's Island and up to the Mayflower Marina, where we were towed to a berth. After a year-and-a-half of preparation and dreaming, *Golden Harp* and I were finally in Plymouth together. I could hardly believe it.

It was now Monday, May 24th, and there were only twelve working days left before the start on Saturday, June 5th. I had carefully planned to be in Plymouth that far ahead to have time to handle any unexpected problems, and a good thing it was, too. My biggest problem was the engine. Actually, the engine in its broken state performed the only function it had to for the race, charging the batteries, but I did not like the idea of having a major piece of equipment not in working order, even if it had to be sealed during the race so that it could not be used as a propellant. Besides, it was still on warranty, and that would have elapsed by the time I arrived in Newport. The plan was for O. H. Rogers, who was driving my car to Plymouth, to bring with him a new tank, which comprised the major part of the hydraulic drive unit. I had described all the symptoms to the Hydromarine people in Galway, and they were sure that it was either the propellor or the tank. I had performed all the tests instructed by both Hydromarine and their agents in Southampton, and they felt it could only be one of the two problems. O.H. should have arrived on the Tuesday, and I had the engineer coming from Southampton on that day, but then O.H. phoned from somewhere in Somerset to say that my car had blown a cylinder head gasket and he would be delayed a day, so the whole operation was put back.

Finally, O.H. arrived with the new tank and the spare propellor pins, and all was ready. The engineer arrived from Southampton, walked under the boat, which we had dried out on the scrubbing pad at the marina, turned the propellor first one way and then the other and said, 'It's not the tank and it's not the propellor; it's the driven pump, which sits behind the tank, and I don't have one with me. Didn't anybody tell you to try turning the propellor both ways? It should only turn one way.' Nobody had mentioned this simple test. The engineer promised to see that the proper parts were sent and instructed a local mechanic on how to perform the relatively simple installation.

O.H. and I pressed on with small jobs, assisted by Peter Adams, a local friend of a friend who was very helpful in getting me around the strange city of Plymouth, and in transporting my Harrod's stores and Avery's wine from the Royal Western office in Millbay Docks to the marina for stowage aboard *Harp*. The arrival of these stores had caused much amusement at the Royal Western. Harrod's had packed everything so carefully that the apparent volume of my food was twice its real volume. There were two huge crates and three cases of wine from Avery's. Nobody could believe the shipment was for thirty-foot *Golden Harp* and not for 236-foot *Club Méditerranée*.

The slaving aboard the boat was relieved by an increasingly active social life as more and more competitors arrived. The bar at the Royal Western was getting more crowded by the day, and nobody talked about *anything* except the Race – especially what equipment different boats were carrying and, most of all, the riddle of which route to take.

There are two main routes taken by most competitors and several variations. The most-sailed route, and the one which had always been sailed by the winning yacht, is the great circle route. Its principle attraction is that it is the shortest, about 2,800 miles. But it has great disadvantages, too: the weather can be very rough at times, there is the likelihood of icebergs and fog along the way and, worst of all, a skipper taking this route must expect headwinds nearly all the way, and he must tack back and forth in order to get west, since a sailboat cannot sail straight into the wind. This circumstance can add several hundred miles to the distance actually sailed.

The second important route is the southern, or Azores route. This involves setting a southwesterly course to and past the Azores, down to about latitude 37° north, then turning west and sailing to about longitude 65° west, before turning northwest for Newport. On the face of it this route sounds silly, since it is about 3,500 miles long, but it does have its advantages. In a year of typical weather, a skipper will have a lot of reaching winds and not nearly so much beating to windward as on the great circle route, and thus should be able to sail much faster. Nobody taking this route had ever won the Race, but in each Race somebody always came close, and often it turned out that boats taking the Azores route sailed fewer miles than boats which had had to tack back and forth on the great circle route. Another major attraction for the Azores route is kinder weather and lots of sunshine and, of course, the Azores themselves are on the route in case a boat suffers damage or her skipper is injured. The big disadvantage of the route is the big Azores High which, in addition to providing sunshine, can also provide extended periods of calm, and sailboats do not sail in calm weather: they sit on the sea, occasionally being pushed in the wrong direction by ocean currents.

There are variations, as I have mentioned: there is a high, northern route, where some hope to pick up following winds, but the risk of ice is much higher; and there is the very southerly trade winds route, which offers almost certain free sailing, but which is so long that it has rarely been taken in the Race. The big joker in the pack is the Gulf Stream, a strong ocean current which originates in the Gulf of Mexico, runs around the tip of Florida, up the east coast of the United States, turns northeast and continues across the Atlantic towards the British Isles. Anyone trying to sail a route between the great circle and the Azores routes will have to contend with this major, adverse current, and most prefer to avoid it, those on the great circle route remaining north of the Stream, and those on the Azores route remaining south of it, until crossing the current almost at right angles when turning northwest for Newport. The excellent chart from the official Race programme is reproduced here and illustrates all the various routes.

Many people had already made the decision to plunge straight across via the great circle, no matter what; others would not consider any route but the Azores. I was undecided, preferring to wait for the weather briefing the day before the Race before making a decision, but I was biased toward the Azores route. *Harp* went well in light moderate airs, and I felt my level of experience was probably better suited to going south.

I had had some advice from the Irish Weather Service, who had kindly sent me some charts and diagrams and reported on some studies of westerly winds in the North Atlantic, but the sum total of all these was that nobody could predict anything about the weather we would encounter with any degree of probability, let alone certainty. So I would wait for the final briefing, in the meantime soliciting as many opinions as possible – and there were almost as many opinions about the route as there were competitors. There was a great deal of caginess in any discussion of route, nobody being willing to commit himself on the

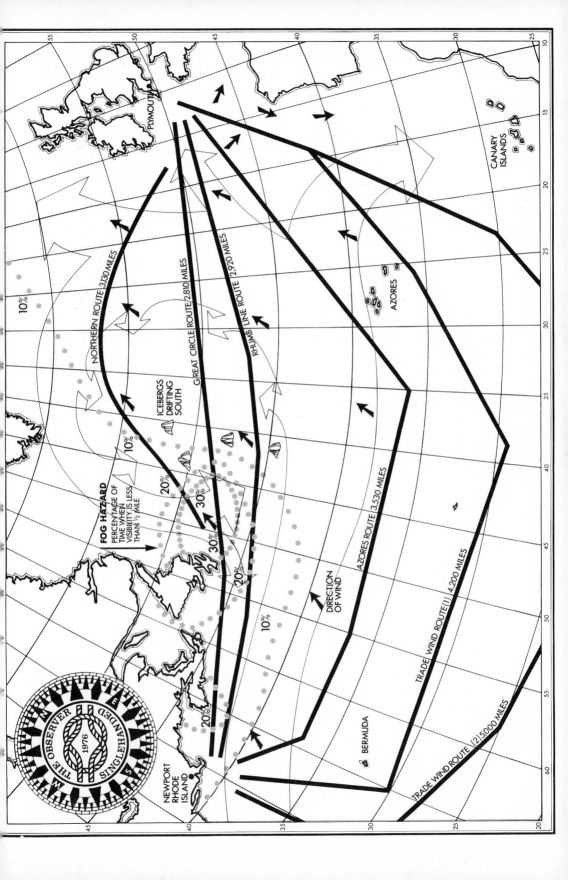

Richard Clifford, relaxed and confident at the start. *Quest* zooms by in the background.

subject. If somebody did commit himself he was probably lying and would be taking another route on the day. This caginess always made me laugh, since the whole question was so riddled with uncertainty and the weather on any route so unpredictable that it seemed to make little difference what anybody thought before the Race.

On Tuesday night, Richard Clifford invited me aboard *Shamaal II*, on which he lived, for drinks. It was a big party for a small boat, comprising Richard, myself, Robert Hughes, the Gibb self-steering expert, two other Royal Marine officers, the Bulgarian entry, Georgi Georgiev, and two people who were to have a large effect on my life, Mike and Lizzie McMullen. Mike was sailing *Three Cheers*, a fast trimaran designed by the very successful Dick Newick. His practice crew, David Hopkins, was also there.

Mike McMullen had sailed *Binkie*, a thirty-two foot monohull, in the last OSTAR and had finished well up. While in Newport he had been invited for a sail on *Three Cheers* by Tom Follett, who had sailed her in the Race. Mike had been instantly attracted to the boat, although he had never sailed a multihull, and bought *Three Cheers* and immediately began to sail her in preparation for the next OSTAR. Lizzie had enthusiastically joined in the project and they had spent a great deal of time together on the boat during the ensuing four years. The previous summer they had made an extended cruise to the Hebrides and made a film about it which was soon to be shown by the BBC. Mike was a tough, former Royal Marines Commando Officer and a superb yachtsman, and his ability, in combination with such a fast and proven boat as *Three Cheers*, had made him one of the favourites to win the Race outright, in spite of the fact that *Three Cheers*, at forty-six feet overall, was much smaller than the other favourites.

I was attracted to Mike and Lizzie McMullen as I have rarely been attracted to any couple, their collective charm, enthusiasm and total commitment to the Race captivating me completely. Mike held forth on his opinions about the OSTAR and Lizzie goaded him from the sidelines; we talked and talked and laughed constantly. Lizzie was a very beautiful girl, and I complimented her on her nose. (There are leg men, etc., etc. I have always been a nose man.) She liked that, and it became our private joke.

We eventually continued the party in the bar of the Royal Western, and by the end of the evening I counted them as close friends, difficult as that may be to explain. For ten days I would see them constantly, then I would not see them again.

Angela Green of the *Observer* arrived to set up the press office, and we began to see a great deal of each other, often meeting Mike and Lizzie in the Club for drinks and another discussion of the Race.

Harry had flown back to Ireland the day after our arrival, and now O.H. had to leave, too, so I was on my own. I greatly envied those entrants who seemed to have whole staffs of people to fetch and carry and bolt things onto their boats. Even some of the smaller boats had vans full of gear and teams of friends, relatives or professionals working on their problems. Ann was coming down the Thursday before the Race, but until then I would have to get help where I could find it. Robert Hughes, in addition to servicing Fred, was most helpful with stowing my food, and Ian Radford, who was in the marina aboard his entry, *Jabulisiwe*, and who was much readier than I, was very helpful. The marina staff did what they could, and Alec Blagdon loaned tools from his boatyard, even though I did not have to take *Harp* there for anticipated repairs. But by the end of the week, although a great deal had been accomplished, my list of things to do did not seem any shorter, and *Harp* would have to be moved into Millbay Docks on Monday night, along with all the other entries, to undergo her three inspections – one for water and stores, one for safety equipment, and one for structural soundness and suitability of gear. She would also have to be inspected by the Handicap Committee, and the gear lever of her engine would be sealed, so that the engine could only be driven in neutral, for battery charging.

In addition to the list of things I had planned to do in Plymouth, new problems kept cropping up: first, the hydraulic drive problem, then the engine's electrical system. An electrical engineer came aboard and immediately found the problem which had caused my batteries to discharge: one of the battery wires had been led across part of the engine's exhaust system which, when it got hot, had burned through the insulation of the wire, causing a short circuit.

On Saturday night Angela and I invited Mike and Lizzie McMullen to come aboard *Harp* for drinks. They were tied up until later in the evening, so Angela and I had dinner at Bella Napoli, which was becoming a sort of culinary headquarters for everybody, and went back to the boat to wait for them. They were late, and as we were sitting below having a drink, we heard a commotion from across the marina. I stuck my head through the hatch and looked around. Two pontoons away a large group of dark figures was gathered around another boat, some of them pounding on the coachroof, others pumping up and down on the bowsprit, pitching the boat fore and aft. I heard someone shout above the din, 'Aha! We know what you're at!' I went back below, laughing, and told Angela that some poor bastard across the way was having either his sleep or his amorous activities disturbed by his friends.

A few moments later I heard hushed puzzled voices on the pontoon next to *Harp* and stuck my head out again to see what was up. Mike and Lizzie and half-a-dozen other people were standing there, trying to figure out where *Golden Harp* was. Forgetting that *Harp* was an Irish entry, they had asked at the marina office for the *American* boat and had been directed to *Catapha*, whose skipper, David White, had been rudely awakened by a great deal of noise and commotion. 'What really worried me,' Mike said, as they all tumbled below and found seats, 'was how *big* that guy was.' Andrew and Roslyn Spedding, close friends of the McMullens, had come along, together with David Hopkins and Paul Weychan, designer and builder of *Quest*, a fast-looking trimaran which would be sailed by John deTrafford. There were a couple of other people jammed into *Harp* as well, but in the ensuing joking and laughing I forgot their names. Andrew Spedding had sailed in the last OSTAR, and was one of the scrutineers who would be inspecting *Harp* in Millbay Docks. I tried to keep his glass full.

At one point in the evening I remember Mike remarking, 'There's a lot of luck involved in this Race.' It was a comment I had not heard anyone else make, and I would have occasion to recall it later.

Book Four
23 Countdown

MONDAY. I spent the morning doing small jobs on the boat. The marina mechanic, Ted, came and changed the engine's water pump, which had been leaking, and installed a new Jabsco electric bilge pump.

Ian Radford volunteered to come with me on the tow to Millbay Docks and help me berth *Harp* there, which might be tricky with no engine and so many boats about. Ian is a young physician who had been practising in Zululand and who had done a stint performing heart surgery with Christian Barnard in South Africa. He had accepted a new job in Miami, Florida, and was emigrating the hard way, via the OSTAR. A cheerful soul, Ian was always ready to lend a hand with no more recompense than a cold beer or two . . . or three.

As we were waiting for the towing vessel to come for us, Lizzie trotted up, a bottle of whisky in each hand, and invited us to come for a look at *Three Cheers*. The lovely, primrose yellow trimaran was tied up at an outer pontoon of the marina, where she had just been blessed by the family vicar. The bottles of booze were gifts from friends who had turned up for the ceremony. Nigel Lang of *Galadrial*, one of the little Contessa 26's in the Race, joined us, and we spent a pleasant half hour aboard as Mike, with obvious pleasure and pride, gave us a Cook's tour of the boat. I had only been on one or two tris, and I was fascinated as Mike explained the modifications he had made which would make her an even faster boat than when Tom Follett had sailed her. I lifted an upside-down bucket in the cabin and found a small Ham-type short-wave radio transmitter. He was keeping the bucket over it, Mike explained, because he had not had time to get a licence for it, and anyway, he would only use it in emergencies. Nigel remarked on the absence of stanchions and guardrails on the boat, but Mike pooh-poohed the idea, saying he thought they were unnecessary.

We finished our tour and Ian and I invited Lizzie to stop by *Harp* for a glass of sherry on her way home, since she was passing the boat, anyway. Lizzie, who had been fascinated with all the little comforts on *Harp* compared to the austerity of the lightweight *Three Cheers,* rolled her eyes and said she'd just *love* to come and see my central heating and listen to my stereo again. I said she could snuggle up to my central heating anytime, and as we left Mike shouted after us, 'You watch that fellow, I don't trust anybody who has central heating and stereo on his boat!' We left *Three Cheers,* Lizzie giggling, and strolled along to *Harp.* We had sat and chatted only for a minute when the towing vessel turned up, and we had to cast off. As Lizzie jumped ashore we agreed that Angela and I would try and meet them at the club later that evening for dinner. 'Don't forget to bring your nose!' I shouted after her as she ran toward the car park, still clutching the whisky.

She laughed and waved the bottle. I was looking forward to spending another evening with the McMullens.

John, the marina's bosun, towed us slowly around to Millbay, and as the gates were not yet open, we had an opportunity to circle and get a close look at *Club Méditerranée.* From the water she seemed even more massive, with her four tall masts, enormous deckhouse and huge windcharger propellor aft. Alongside her, *Golden Harp* looked about the same size as the little Avon dinghy we were towing looked alongside *Harp.* As we waited for the car ferry from France to dock and the Millbay gates to open, other yachts began to congregate in the area, and by the time the gates opened a dozen or more boats of all sizes were there, this being the final deadline for entering the docks without incurring a time penalty.

Inside, Captain Terence Shaw, former Secretary of the Royal Western, who was in charge of docking arrangements, directed us to a berth alongside *Pawn of Nieuwpoort,* being sailed by the Belgian entrant, Yves Anrys, and *Achille,* whose skipper was the young Frenchman, Max Bourgeois. Terence Shaw, white-bearded and very salty-looking, did not need a megaphone to issue his instructions, and skippers disregarded them at their peril. Soon, Nigel Lang, in *Galadrial* and young Simon Hunter, in *Kylie,* another Contessa 26, were tied up outside us, making a raft of five boats, with *Achille* closest to the concrete dockside.

Behind us were the two Chinese lugsail schooners, *Ron Glas* (which is Gaelic for grey seal), sailed by Jock McCleod, a Scot, and Bill King's old boat, *Galway Blazer II,* now owned by Peter Crowther, who is just a bit mad. Also there was Angus Primrose in a Moody 33 of his own design, *Demon Demo,* soon joined by Chris Smith in the tiny *Tumult,*

Lizzie and Mike McMullen.

Three Cheers under full sail.

only twenty-two feet long.

Millbay Docks was now home to nearly every boat that would start, and the whole place took on a festive air that completely changed the ordinarily drab appearance of the place. Angela and her *Observer* press office were there; Camper & Nicholson's and M. S. Gibb were sharing a portabuilding, and Brookes & Gatehouse were located in a trailer nearby. All the famous boats from past races were there: *Jester*, the Chinese lugsail folkboat which had been sailed in every OSTAR, first by Blondie Hasler and later by Michael Richey; *Tahiti Bill*, Bill Howell's cat; *Vendredi Treize*, the 128-foot giant of the last Race, now called *ITT Oceanic*; *Cap 33*, formerly a French trimaran, now sailed by an American from Boston, Tom Grossman. *Manureva*, in which Alain Colas had won the last Race, was to have been sailed by his brother, but had lost a float and would not compete.

Among the new boats were *Kriter III*, a seventy-foot catamaran built as *British Oxygen*, winner of the Round Britain Race when sailed by Robin Knox-Johnston (beating Mike McMullen in the much smaller *Three Cheers* by less than an hour); *Pen Duick VI*, Eric Tabarly's boat, built to be sailed in the Round-the-World Race by a crew of fifteen, now being sailed by Tabarly alone; *Galloping Gael*, a boat designed to the maximum limit of the *Jester* class and sailed by an Irish/Canadian/American, Mike Flanagan; *FT*, also designed to the maximum of the smallest class and sailed by David Palmer, who seemed certain he would take the class prize; *Spaniel*, a hitherto unknown Polish entry, with a bucket seat and automotive steering wheel in her tiny deckhouse; five identical boats designed by Marc Linski, a Frenchman, and four identical thirty-two foot trimarans designed by Dick Newick especially for the Race, one of them sailed by a close friend of Ron Holland's, Walter Green, an American.

With the withdrawal of *Great Britain III* and *Manureva*, only seven boats were entered in the largest group, the *Pen Duick* class. One of the most interesting was a sixty-two foot trimaran with a truly vast sail area, *Spirit of America*, sailed by Mike Kane, who claimed his boat to be the fastest multihull in the world. The medium-sized *Gypsy Moth* class had considerably more entrants, but by far the largest was the *Jester* class, with about ninety boats, most of them privately owned, non-sponsored boats like *Harp*.

Living conditions not being in the category of wonderful in Millbay Docks, I moved into a hotel until the start. On Monday night Angela and I went to a party given by Tom Grossman of *Cap 33* and met a number of other entrants. Although we knew each other by sight, this was my first meeting with Mike Kane. He was reputed to be a bit cocky

'No pictures, please.' Mike Kane of
Spirit of America.

Tahiti Bill Howell.

about his boat and his chances, and with a few drinks under his belt he was in rare form, talking about the incredible speeds the Lock Crowther-designed tri could reach and how well-proven she was. We lingered a bit too long among the congenial company at Tom's party and missed Mike and Lizzie at the Club.

TUESDAY. The hydraulic engineer rang and said that Hydromarine would reluctantly supply the needed replacement unit, but that they were insisting he come back and install it. I cringed at the cost, but I agreed. I spent the morning rounding up bits and pieces of gear, including two white fishing floats which would have to be painted black to conform to a last-minute rule that each yacht carry two black balls hoisted when the boat was under self-steering with no one on deck, a concession to the criticism from *Yachting World*. I was doing this job when the first of the scrutineers, Walter Venning, arrived aboard *Harp*. 'Come aboard,' I said. 'I was just painting my balls black.' Then from behind him appeared his girl friend, Sally, the other scrutineer. I think I blushed.

They asked to see all the required safety equipment, checking each item off on a list, then chatted for a minute. Walter turned out to be a cousin of Bill King's, whom Bill had told me about. He is a tomato grower and once, when Bill was about to make a transatlantic crossing in his first boat, *Galway Blazer I*, Walter gave him a basket of tomatoes which had been carefully selected so that one of them would ripen each day. It had worked perfectly, Bill said, the last tomato ripening on his last day out.

Yves Anrys and I had a chance to talk a lot as we were each doing jobs on our boats. Yves had been a reserve Olympic helmsman in the

Yves Anrys of *Pawn of Nieuwpoort,*
Harp's next-door neighbour in Millbay
Dock.

Angus Primrose

singlehanded Finn dinghy class and was sailing a half-tonner similar to
Harp, but very stripped-out inside and much, much lighter. He is a
merchant seaman and was planning to race his boat in the World Half-
Ton Cup Championships later in the year.

WEDNESDAY. I was a blur of motion all the morning, running errands,
seeing to last-minute fittings and filling small gaps in my list of
necessary gear. There seemed to be no end to it, and I was beginning to
have a feeling of running out of time. While in this somewhat harassed
state I got a telephone message from the Royal Western office in Millbay
Docks that the McWilliams and the Hollands were arriving at four in
the afternoon and please to meet them.

We arrived back at Millbay Docks and were standing outside the
Observer press office chatting with some people, when Angela called me
aside. 'Have you heard about Lizzie McMullen?' she asked. Oh God, I
thought, there's been a car crash and Lizzie's in hospital with a broken
leg or something.

'No,' I said.

'There's been a terrible accident. Mike and Lizzie were working on the boat at Mashford's yard this morning when an electric drill fell overboard into the water. Mike shouted for her not to touch it, but she did. They gave her heart massage and artificial respiration for half-an-hour until an ambulance could get out to Cremyl, but it didn't help. She was dead on arrival at the hospital.'

I froze inside; I couldn't believe what she was telling me. Lizzie McMullen, beautiful, bright, delightful Lizzie could not be dead; it was simply not possible. I asked Angela if she were absolutely sure, if there were any possibility of a mistake. Angela was sure. Lizzie, who thirty-six hours before had been joking about my central heating, laughing and sipping sherry on *Golden Harp* was gone. Irrecoverable. Out of anyone's reach. Out of my life. Out of Mike's. Dear God, I thought, if I feel this way, as if somebody had struck me with a blunt instrument, how must Mike feel?

'How is Mike?' I asked Angela.

'I don't know. I'm sure friends are with him. I've sent a telegram.' I wanted to send a telegram, too. I sat in Angela's office and thought for a time. There were less than seventy-two hours left before the start of the Race. This would have been the most crushing possible blow at any time, but to happen now, after four years of work and preparation *together*. It suddenly seemed unthinkable that Mike should not sail the Race. I found a pencil and wrote, 'I only knew her for a week, and I loved her, too. There is no answer to the senseless. Please sail the Race and win it.' I signed the telegram, gave it to Angela to send, then went out and sat in the car, numb. A man wandered over and began talking to me through the open sunroof about an ice cream seller who had been ejected from the docks because he didn't have the proper permit. I chatted absently with him without knowing what I was saying. Angela came out and we talked for a moment, then I left. I felt I had to keep doing things, that I couldn't stop – not just because I had so much to get done, but because if I stopped I would think about Lizzie and, worse, about Mike. So I kept moving, kept ticking items off my list, but it seemed that every two or three minutes I would stop and realize all over again that Lizzie was dead, and it was just like being told for the first time.

I spent most of the afternoon with the Hollands and McWilliams, but in a kind of daze. When they left for the airport early that evening, I went to the Club. I found Lloyd Foster and asked if he knew Mike's plans about the Race. 'I think it will certainly be impossible for Mike to compete now,' he said. 'Of course, there's the funeral, but there'll have to be an inquest as well. There are just too many formalities to complete before Saturday.' I suggested that the competitors might send some flowers, and Lloyd agreed to receive contributions. Later, that didn't seem enough, seemed too transient, and some of us thought perhaps the Committee might accept a new trophy for multihulls to be presented in memory of Lizzie. This seemed much more satisfactory, more permanent, and Lloyd said he would bring it before the Committee for consideration.

I don't think anyone who knew Lizzie McMullen, however slightly, went to bed with dry eyes that night, and I was more deeply affected than at any time since my grandfather had died. It had been a bad day. THURSDAY. Everything began to gather momentum. There were three events scheduled for competitors: a Lord Mayor's reception at midday, a competitors' briefing in the early afternoon and a dinner that evening. In between, I was at a dead run. The hydraulics engineer from Southampton turned up bright and early with the new pump. I spent the rest of the morning running errands and arrived at the Lord Mayor's event after the speeches. Lloyd Foster called me over to confer with Henry Williams and Col. Jack Oddling-Smee of the Committee, who agreed to accept the proposed Lizzie trophy. Liz Balcon of *The Observer* voiced the newspaper's approval, and both the Club and *The Observer* agreed to contribute a substantial amount of money to be combined with the competitors' contributions to purchase a piece of silver. Lloyd asked me to announce the trophy at the competitors' briefing in the afternoon and said he would accept the contributions.

I found Richard Clifford chatting with a very attractive girl and the three of us adjourned to a local restaurant for an hour to rest from the rush of the day. Richard told me that Mike had decided to continue in the Race and would be at the briefing. I felt vastly relieved and very happy about that. Yves Anrys had said to me the previous afternoon, 'The man's wife is dead, that's one problem. If he doesn't do the Race he will have two problems.' I thought that described the situation very succinctly, and I was glad that Mike would not have to suffer the additional agony of missing the Race. I hoped, too, that competing might have a therapeutic effect.

As we gathered at the Royal Western for a group photograph and the briefing, I found Mike, looking shattered but holding up well, told him what we wanted to do and asked if he minded if it were announced at the briefing. He agreed readily. When we sat down for the photograph on the Club's front terrace, there seemed to be a thousand photographers, and I think most of us were a little taken aback at all the attention, not being used to that sort of thing. I was sitting somewhere near Clare Francis and the crush around us was incredible as all the photographers, as one man, rushed forward for close-ups of the prettiest skipper in the Race. A lot of attention was focused on Mike, too, but this was more discreet, thankfully. We filed into the main lounge of the Club and were briefed on the starting and finishing procedures; the *Pen Duick* Class would start at twelve noon, the *Gypsy Moth* Class at twelve-thirty and the *Jester* Class at one o'clock. The finishing line would be a line between the Brenton Reef lighthouse and a nearby buoy, and we were given a chart of the Newport area. A representative of the Ida Lewis Yacht Club of Newport, who was handling the arrangements at the other end, said that an effort would be made to meet as many competitors as possible. Other details were discussed, then I made the announcement about the new prize, to be called The Lizzie McMullen Perpetual Trophy, for the first multihull to finish. It would be a presentation of the competitors in the 1976 Race and would be presented in perpetuity. There were a few more announcements and we broke up to return to our boats.

Ann arrived during the afternoon, and I left her to rest at the hotel while I got back to the boat. Arriving there, I found that the replacement hydraulic unit had blown immediately upon installation, and the engineer was trying to cannibalize the old unit to repair the new one. I got the electrical engineer started on replacing the battery and rewiring the engine bay, working around the other engineer as best he could. This was a time when I had planned to be lounging in the cockpit with a glass of wine, watching everybody else panic. Instead, Yves Anrys was lounging in *his* cockpit, watching *me* panic. The Handicap Committee came by and had a look at *Harp*. I sat them down and explained as thoroughly as I could that *Harp* was *not* in her present condition a competitive half-tonner, that she was much, much too heavy for that and had larger rigging, steps on the mast and lots of other windage-making gear, such as the Dynafurl reefing. They nodded sympathetically and agreed that she would not rate as a standard half-tonner, and I felt I had made my point successfully.

I raced back to the hotel to change for the banquet, and we made it on time. The atmosphere was relaxed, and although a lot of people looked tired, as I'm sure I did, everybody looked happy. Ann got her bottom pinched by somebody who turned out to be Jerry Cartwright, an American yacht designer from Newport and a friend of Ron's. I asked her if she wanted me to hit him, but she seemed flattered.

We sat with Yves Anrys, Max Bourgeois and Ian Radford, with Bill Howell at the next table, so we were among friends. Jack Oddling-Smee made a gracious and amusing speech, the new editor of *The Observer*, the incredibly young-looking Donald Trelford, made another and Val

Howells responded on behalf of the competitors. Val had been a competitor in the first Race, in 1960, and now he and his son Philip had built identical boats for the *Jester* class for this Race. The party broke up and everybody went to get some sleep before the last full day we would have before the start.

FRIDAY. We were up at the crack of dawn and back on the boat. The two engineers were working away at it, and I sent Ann off in the car for some last-minute shopping, while I worked on the boat. With the two engineers still working it was a mess, and with only a day to go.

Lizzie McMullen was buried in the family plot at the little church in the Cornish village of St Mellion, a few miles from Plymouth. Mike Kane and I drove up, and Richard Clifford and Clare Francis were there, too. Mike McMullen bore himself in a manner which put us all to shame. 'He's taking it better than I am,' Mike Kane said.

Mike invited us back to the house after the funeral, and was everywhere, putting everybody at ease. He showed us around the place, a pair of workmen's cottages he and Lizzie had been converting into a single house, doing all the work themselves. Only one room was completely finished, and it was heartbreaking to see, on a beautiful Cornish hillside with a view nearly to Plymouth, still another project that they had begun but would not finish together. I told Mike how glad I was that he would be sailing the Race. He said, 'Your telegram just about did it, you know.' I said I thought Lizzie would have been pleased, too, and Lizzie's father, who was standing with us, agreed.

On the drive back to Plymouth, Mike Kane and I got to know each other better, and I began to appreciate the pressures he was under, over and above anything I was experiencing. He was being sponsored by the American Tobacco Company, and a crew had been sent to make a film about his project. A camera and sound crew were following him around everywhere he went; they had been in California taking shots of his home and family before he left for England, and there were the usual PR men skating him around the TV and press people, too. He was longing to be out at sea, I think, leaving it all behind.

Ann and I worked the rest of the day stowing gear and tidying up last-minute details. By early evening *Harp* was nearly ready. During the afternoon I met Mike Flanagan of *Galloping Gael*; he came aboard, introduced himself and asked to borrow my dinghy to do some work on the topsides of his boat. I had heard that Mike was very confident of his chances in the *Jester* class and wasn't shy about it. We chatted for a couple of minutes, and he seemed a nice enough guy.

Mike Kane came to the dockside, camera crew in tow, and we had a shouted exchange of good-natured abuse for the benefit of the television

Club Méditerranée and *Golden Harp* to scale

audience. Robert Hughes arrived and replaced the steering vane shaft which had been bent in the altercation with the customs launch in St Mawes. Everything was finally aboard and fitted; only some stowage remained, and we left that for the following morning.

Ann and I had hoped to have a farewell dinner at the superb Horn of Plenty in Gulworthy, but we finished on the boat too late and decided on dinner at Bella Napoli after a drink at the Royal Western. There we bumped into Jerry Cartwright, the well-known yacht designer and bottom pincher, and a very attractive English girl, Suzy Wassman, who had lived for a time in Newport. They joined us for dinner. Jerry had done the last OSTAR, but hadn't been able to complete a boat in time for this one, and we talked all through dinner about the Race, the routes and problems I might encounter. I had missed most of the weather briefing that afternoon, turning up at the wrong place, but everybody I talked to still seemed to think it was a toss-up between routes. Only a smaller-than-usual amount of ice on the great circle made that route seem a possible favourite. I was still leaning toward the Azores route, having heard nothing new against it, but still had not made a final decision. I would not really have to do that until leaving the Channel.

I was also bitching a lot about the handicap I had been assigned that afternoon. Nobody knew what handicapping system the Committee was using, but whatever it was, I didn't like it. *Harp* had been given a handicap of nineteen days and some hours; *Pawn of Nieuwpoort*, Yves Anrys' boat, identical in size to *Harp*, but stripped out inside and much lighter, had been assigned a handicap of twenty-two days and some hours. I was giving Yves three days! Clare Francis, in her thirty-eight foot *Robertson's Golly*, was giving me only half-a-day! When Yves and I sat down and went through the list, we discovered still more strangeness. *Harp*, designed as a half-tonner, was actually giving time to a one-tonner! I had written out an immediate protest to the Committee, citing half-a-dozen apparent anomalies, and they had told me I would get a decision in Newport. I was very concerned about this, because the handicap prize was the only one *Harp* had any real chance of winning, being eight feet overall and three-and-a-half feet on the waterline shorter than the class maximum.

In spite of all the shop talk, the pleasant dinner eased the tension a bit and, since Jerry would be on the press boat at the start, we invited Suzy to join Ann and me on *Harp* for the time before the start. That way she could get inside the restricted zone, where spectator craft were not allowed.

Tomorrow was the day, but I was too tired at bedtime to reflect much about it.

SATURDAY AND THE START. We were up at six, collected my fresh meat, a week's supply, from the hotel freezer, where it had not frozen, stopped by the fish market for a large bag of ice, which smelled like fish, and got down to the boat. I dropped Ann, the meat and the fishy ice there and drove to the marina, where Mike Kane had promised me some last-minute weather poop. Mike was late and I had too much to do to wait, so I went back to Millbay Docks, giving Richard Konkolski, the Czech entry, a lift. I hadn't had an opportunity to talk with Richard before, but he was an interesting fellow, sailing his little, home-built twenty-four-footer, *Nike*, in the Race for the second time. Since the Czechs have no boat-building industry and import restrictions abound, Richard had had to build his boat from whatever materials he could find, making many fittings himself, even the sails.

Since repairs on *Harp*'s engine had been completed so late, there had been no opportunity for the Committee to seal the gear lever, and I was given an acceptance certificate and told they would trust me. (As it turned out, they didn't have to.) This meant that, unlike the other competitors, we had a useable engine for the period before the start and did not have to be towed. So, with Ann and Suzy aboard, we were among the first out of the docks, collecting a round of applause from the crowd gathered at the gates. (Angela told me later that *all* the competitors got a round of applause. I had thought it was just for *me*.)

We motored out to the starting area, stowing gear all the while, and started to look at boats. I don't think anybody got a better look at things than we, with our engine. We motored back and forth through the fleet, dodging hundreds of spectators that could simply not be kept out of the restricted area, in spite of the best efforts of the Royal Marines, buzzing about in inflatable assault craft, yelling at people. There was every possible kind of spectator boat inside the restricted area, most of them small yachts under power, but I even saw two kids in a Mirror dinghy thrashing about among the competitors.

In spite of what sounds like chaotic conditions, everything was quite orderly, the spectators were well-behaved, apart from their trespassing, and I did not see a single incident of any kind. Fortunately, it was a light day. In heavy weather things would have been a bit hairier, but then, in heavy weather, there would not have been so many spectators.

Club Méditerranée sailed slowly around at the starboard end of the line, her decks crawling with people (spectators did not have to be off the boats until the ten-minute gun), and *Spirit of America* stayed nearby. I knew Mike Kane wanted badly to start before Colas, and there he was, waiting.

The ten-minute gun went for the big class, and the huge boats started jockeying for position. *ITT Oceanic*, sailed by Yvon Fauconnier, was down at the starboard end of the line with *Club Med* and *Spirit*, and the other large boats were more scattered. Poor Tom Grossman, on *Cap 33*, had been bumped up from the *Gypsy Moth* to the *Pen Duick* class when it was found that his boat exceeded the length for the medium class. He had simply taken the word of the previous owner on her measurements, and now he was in with the big boys, the smallest boat in the class.

Seconds before the gun I saw Mike Kane get *Spirit* into irons nearly on top of the starting line. He just stood in the cockpit shaking both fists in the air until the big tri decided which tack she wanted. Fortunately for Mike, Colas was late, and *Spirit* recovered in time to nip *Club Med* at the line. Then *Spirit* was gone, revelling in the light conditions, while *Club Med* moved sluggishly towards the Channel. It was clear that if it were going to be a light-weather race Mike would probably win it hands down.

Mike McMullen sailed past in *Three Cheers*, and I shouted to him, 'Win it, Mike!'

'I'll bloody well try!' he shouted back. He was smiling.

As soon as the *Gypsy Moth* bunch were away I put Ann and Suzy off onto a spectator boat, switched off the engine and began to sail slowly around under main only, the reefing genoa furled, and the drifter lashed on deck in case the wind dropped. I have never experienced anything quite like the atmosphere among the competitors at the starting line. Here, in an intensely competitive situation, everybody was wishing everybody else luck! Each time two boats passed there were shouts, jokes and absurd insults exchanged. I saw and exchanged greetings with Nigel Lang, Ian Radford, Max Bourgeois, Peter Crowther, Angus Primrose, Andrew Bray, Richard Konkolski, Richard Clifford, Ziggy Puchalski, Mike Flanagan, Simon Hunter and two dozen or so others whom I had never met, but were wishing me luck, anyway.

I saw Angela, aboard one of the *Observer* press boats, and waved goodbye. We were planning to meet in Newport, where she would be running another press office at the other end. I saw the boat carrying Ann and Suzy a couple of times more, and then I heard the ten-minute gun. I had chosen the starboard end of the line, because starting on the starboard tack would give me right of way over boats on the port tack. I ignored all other tactical considerations in favour of playing it as safely as possible. With nearly ninety boats on the line it would be all too easy to collide with somebody and be out of the Race with damage before it even started. In spite of my decision to play it safe, though, I felt all my dinghy racing instincts coming back as the minutes ticked away; I stopped thinking about safety and started thinking how to be on the line when the gun went. Suddenly, nothing else mattered.

I made a couple of passes at the line under main only, then settled into an oval pattern near the starboard end, gybing around in circles and watching my stopwatch. At about a minute-and-a-half to go, I found myself being crowded by the Linski boats, all five of them, who seemed determined to start as a fleet. At forty-five seconds I let go the tiller and hauled on the leeward sheet, breaking out the reefing genoa, and started for the line. I crossed exactly thirty seconds late. Lousy for a dinghy start, but pretty good under these conditions. Much better yachtsmen than I started way behind me.

Nineteen months, almost to the day, after my first offshore passage in a yacht, I was starting across the Atlantic, singlehanded. I felt as if I would explode. I felt terrific.

Spirit of America nips *Club Med.* at the line as *ITT Oceanic* prepares to tack.

SEE OVER: *ITT Oceanic* and *Club Med.* jockey for position at the start, as much as one can jockey for position in boats of this size.

24 At sea at last

As I crossed the line I overtook and sailed between Richard Konkolski in *Nike* and Michael Richey in *Jester*, with only a few feet to spare on either side. After that I was in the clear and had only to worry about yachts approaching on the port tack. I was making about three knots in the light breeze, very good considering *Harp* was wearing the number two genoa instead of the number one. I had set the smaller sail at the start because it would be more manageable in tight quarters.

I sailed perhaps three miles into the Channel in order to lay Penlee Point with plenty of room to spare, noticing that I seemed to be sailing as fast as Clare Francis in *Robertson's Golly*, which was carrying a bigger sail. Just before I tacked, Walter Green in the Dick Newick tri, *Friends*, sailed across my bows, moving very fast. Conditions were ideal for the trimarans and shortly after I tacked, David Palmer in *FT* overtook me to leeward, having apparently got a very bad start. Just after we crossed the line, Peter Adams and his family motored alongside in their small yacht and we made our goodbyes. Now another familiar yacht, *Ruinette*, from Cork, called me on the VHF and wished me luck. It was my last such contact that day, and I felt I was really on my way.

Up to windward Yves Anrys in *Pawn* and Lars Wallgren in *Swedelady* were giving me a boat for boat race. Yves, with his big genoa set, began to pull away from us, and *Swedelady* began to change up to a bigger sail. I hung on to the number two, hoping the wind would freshen, and Yves pulled away from me. Then Ian Radford in *Jabuliswe* appeared astern and began, very slowly, to overtake me. She was a smaller boat than *Harp*, and I knew if I didn't get more wind soon I would have to make the sail change. Because of the furling gear, this was a more difficult change than with conventional gear, and I dreaded losing the time without a foresail during the change. In higher winds when a smaller sail was needed I would have the advantage, but at the moment, in about a Force three, I did not. Ian was right forward in the pulpit of his boat and stayed there for a long time, apparently making some repair.

Then the wind dropped a bit, and I had no choice but to make the sail change. Once Big Jenny, as I called the number one, was up, our boat speed increased and we were making a good four knots. Then the wind freshened again and we did even better. About five in the afternoon, off Fowey, we overtook Angus Primrose in *Demon Demo*, a bigger boat, and I knew we were doing well. Ron had said that *Harp* would do better than the Moody 33 on any point of sailing except reaching, and it appeared he was right. Shortly after that, David Pyle in *Westward*, one of Angus' Moody 30's, just nipped me, but when I tacked again I saw that I was pointing much higher than he, and later I was sure that we had overtaken him.

Darkness fell and there were lights everywhere. There was one yacht in particular that seemed to be keeping pace with us and I thought it must be Ian, in his smaller, but much lighter boat. Nobody could sleep that night while we were still in danger of colliding with each other or with shipping in the Channel.

I drank coffee to keep awake, although I had some Dexadrene should I need it, and dined on ham sandwiches and chilli con carne that Ann had made in Plymouth. In fact, with a dozen sandwiches and a large pot of the chilli, I ate little else for the first three days, except cereal for breakfast. I saw very little shipping, but there were yachts all around us.

At midnight I called Lizard Coast Guard to check the visibility there and was told it was eight hundred yards. By two a.m. it was down to two hundred, but it must have lifted, because I saw the Lizard light briefly at three a.m., then it disappeared. When dawn came, I could see only two yachts as we approached the Lizard, and they soon disappeared after tacking. I did not know it then, but they were the last I would see. The Lizard was really socked in, although visibility on the water seemed about a mile. I came close enough to the headland to hear the fog signal, but I never saw the land at all. It would be some time before I saw any land again.

I tacked away from the Lizard, got the yacht on course and began making telephone calls on the VHF. It was my last chance to say goodbye to people before I was out of range of Land's End radio. It was still very early morning in the Channel, but in the States it was five hours later. I heard a British warship on the VHF to somebody, reporting that some of the larger yachts had been reported at the Scillies, and I chatted with Andrew Bray on *Gillygaloo*. We arranged a calling schedule for noon GMT, but I slept through two of the appointments, and we did not make contact again. I talked with *Chica Boba*, an Italian yacht, which was apparently behind me. Andrew had been ahead. Late in the afternoon I spotted a Scottish yacht, *Sundancer*, not a competitor, called him up and was told that he had seen *FT* near Bishop Rock, which indicated to me that David Palmer was disregarding his earlier, hotly declared intention to go south.

A large group of dolphins came and played with us for half-an-hour or so, then darkness fell again and I faced my second night without sleep. At midnight I heard a very clear VHF transmission from a ship called *Arctic Seal*, who was talking with the coast guard. When his transmission was finished I called him up and had a long, friendly conversation with the officer on watch, Jerry Miller of Port Arthur, Texas. I could see the brightly-lit ship several miles off my port beam and he reported that he could see me on radar at a distance of eight miles, and could see my masthead light as well. This was most comforting. He also gave me a very precise position from his satellite navigational system, which amused me, since Alain Colas had not been permitted to carry that equipment on *Club Med* and had shown a good deal of annoyance towards the perfidious British because of it. I had been able to see *Club Med* for a large part of the first afternoon, and I knew she could not be liking these conditions. I said goodbye to *Arctic Seal* and set a course for the southwest, having made my decision to take the Azores route.

I caught a cold. Coming down the Channel, my throat had become sore and now the whole thing blossomed. This, combined with some queasiness from the rough seas we had begun to experience, made my first week out very uncomfortable. I had little energy and what I had went quickly when I had to deal with some problem, like when the Big Jenny wrapped herself around the forestay. It was worse than the spinnaker wrap had been on the Azores trip, and took a lot longer to get undone.

I was still in radio contact with Land's End and St Mary's coast guard at the freakish distance of 110 miles out, although I could read them better than they me. I tried to relay a message from Lizard coast guard to *FT* about this time, but couldn't raise him. This reinforced my belief that he had gone further north than I.

My radar detector seemed to work, waking me in the middle of the night once, when a big merchant ship went by. Trouble was, it detected other things, too, like my electric razor, and often came on when the boat was being tossed about. Still, it seemed better than not having the thing at all.

I learned the hard way that no sail could be lashed on deck on the leeward side in any kind of a sea, or even on the windward side when things were rough, without its going overboard. This happened twice, but since the sails were shackled onto the deck at the tack, they were recoverable. It was not nearly so tough to get them back on board in a Force seven as it had been in the Force ten coming back from Horta, but it wasn't a hell of a lot of fun, either, and with the cold sapping my strength, it was exhausting.

We were constantly in fresh winds, usually Force five to seven, and sometimes sailing free, so our daily averages were usually a hundred miles or better at this point in the Race, and I felt good about the possibility of achieving my twenty-nine day goal.

My only brush with the opposite sex at sea, a few dolphins apart, came when I raised the German merchant ship *St Clemens* on the VHF and found, to my delight, that she had a female radio operator, one Heidi Riedel. Heidi and I chatted for ten to fifteen minutes, both regretting that we could not get together for a drink. She was from Hamburg and promised to take a message to an old friend there for me. It was the last leisurely radio conversation I would have with anybody, because soon after that when I switched on the ignition to charge the batteries, the engine would not start. The trouble was clearly electrical, and among all the things I did not do well, electrics ranked high. I removed the switch panel, checked all the wiring and sprayed everything with some stuff which was supposed to dispel moisture and improve electrical connections, but nothing. I checked all the connections on the starter motor and sprayed those. Still nothing. I tried jumping the electrics with a screwdriver blade, but succeeded only in making a lot of sparks and frightening myself. Finally, all my electrical ideas exhausted, I tried starting the engine with the hand crank. The manual said this was easy to do, even in cold weather. Ho, ho. I cranked the bloody thing until I couldn't stand up any more, a marline spike stuck under an alternator belt to control the decompression lever. I'd get it spinning well enough, but as soon as I released the decompression lever the engine would stop turning. I thought perhaps a stronger man might turn it further, but I doubted it.

This was a depressing situation, because it meant that when the charge remaining in the batteries was exhausted there would be no electrical power left on the yacht. This would mean no VHF, no cabin lights, no instruments, no stereo tape and, worst of all, no navigation lights. I would still have radio reception for weather reports, radio direction finding and entertainment on the battery-operated Brookes & Gatehouse and Zenith radios, and depth sounding on the battery-operated Seafarer, but no log for speed and mileage recording, no wind direction or wind speed, and no off-course computing from the Hadrian.

I had gone to such pains to ensure that I had the best possible battery charging system, extra-large batteries, two alternators, etc., and now here I was without electrical power because I could not start the engine, a possibility that had never occurred to me. A thousand pounds worth of electrical and electronic equipment was now useless. I went over the whole system again, afraid that I would arrive in Newport, somebody would point at a loose wire and say, 'That's your problem'. There was nothing loose, and apart from that I didn't know where to begin. I stopped using everything electrical except the log.

There had been a shortage of sun for the last few days, and I had been proceeding without sun sights to fix my position. Now, as the remaining charge in my batteries faded away, I knew I would soon be without the log, valuable for keeping a good dead reckoning position. Finally, the log ground out its last hundredth of a mile and stopped. I was left with only those navigational aids which mariners had used for centuries: the compass and the sextant.

I had been at sea for eight days when I got the first bad news. Dominique Berthier, one of the two French girls competing, had lost her yacht, *5100*, but had been rescued by a French trawler. I wondered how she could have been near a trawler after eight days at sea, far from the continental shelf. *(Later information: Mlle Berthier had collided with an unknown cargo carrier and received damage to the yacht's hull. The boat started to take a lot of water and she decided to return to Brest. Nearing France, just off Seil Island, the hull began to break up and she abandoned the yacht for the liferaft, watching the boat sink twenty minutes later. Shortly after that she was taken aboard by the trawler and was in Dovarnenez by midnight.)*

I had finally found the radio frequency for the special weather forecast being broadcast for us by the BBC World Service and what I was hearing sounded very bad for the yachts on the more northern routes. Confirming this, I heard the wife of Guy Hornett, who was sailing *Old Moore's Almanac*, on the Jimmy Young Show on Radio Two; she said Guy had run into two successive Force nine severe gales. Later in the day the BBC reported that Pierre Fehlmann on *Gauloise* had begun taking water and had retired, and that Yvon Fauconnier on *ITT Oceanic* (formerly *Vendredi Treize*) had broken an arm and that some of his sails were in the water. Jock Brazier, in *Flying Angel*, was also reported to have retired with self-steering problems, and H. G. Mitchell in *Tuloa* was said to have retired. That made five that I *knew* about. What else was happening up there? *(Later information: Pierre Fehlmann lost 'Gauloise', and was taken off by another ship under very trying circumstances; Fauconnier and 'ITT' were taken in tow by a Russian tug; Guy Hornett and Harry Mitchell finished the Race.)*

For three days I was in very thick fog with light headwinds, a very bad combination. I could see nothing, and nothing could see me, but at least there was the consolation that merchant ships would be using their radar, and I had a large radar reflector mounted fifteen feet up on the backstay. In fact, it might be easier to detect my presence that way than by eye, especially at night. My daily average began to drop as I tacked through the soup in the light winds. I did some figuring that at my present rate it would take me forty-three days to finish. That was a horrible thought, but I felt it couldn't go on forever like that, and that we would get reaching winds after the Azores and the turn west. After freshening and freeing us for a few hours, the wind went light again and back on the nose. To make matters worse, there was a very large swell running, the product, I suppose, of the rougher weather further north. This made it very difficult to take advantage of what little wind there was. I had set the drifter, the superlight nylon genoa, but the violent motion of the boat shook the light breeze from the sails and the boom swung back and forth and had to be tied. It is one thing to sit on a flat sea with no wind. It is quite another to roll about with no wind. Cooking became messy; messier, even, than in rough weather, when there is a kind of rhythm to the seas. I spilled a glass of red wine all over the tennis whites I was wearing and into my bunk. I got even more bruised than in heavy weather, especially around the knees and thighs, from bumping into things.

During the days, I read as much as I could, finishing Alistair Cook's *America* and starting a biography of Thomas Jefferson. In between, I finished Rosie Swale's *Children of Cape Horn*. Rosie had swept through Plymouth, relieving me of £5 for her club of supporters building the Swale's new catamaran and leaving me with copies of her two books. I ate well. A lunch might include *pâté de canard*, parmesan cheese (with the mould sliced off), Bath Oliver biscuits and half a bottle of Batard Montrachet. I gained weight. I began to cultivate a moustache.

From the radio news I learned that *Kriter III*, formerly *British Oxygen*, was reported to be breaking up and *Club Méditerranée* had been hove-to for three days, repairing sails. There had been a rumour in Plymouth that Colas could not hoist the sails alone, which meant that if he reefed in heavy weather he would not be able to get them up again. I found it difficult to believe that Colas would put himself in that situation, but the word was that there were no winches available big

'Water, water everywhere. . .' Becalmed in mid-Atlantic.

enough for one man to hoist such a huge sail. Somebody else, I didn't get the name, had been picked up in a liferaft.

Then came the really stunning news: there were only ninety-nine competitors left in the Race. Thirty-one had retired or been lost. I had, up until this time, heard about only six or seven boats. Thirty-one gone, and it was June 18th – thirteen days after the start of the Race! A report came that the Soviet tug, *Bestroshryy*, which had taken *ITT* in tow, had also taken Yves Terlain off *Kriter*. He had been able to hold the huge cat together just long enough for help to arrive. Tabarly was reported 850 miles from Newport and it was said that he might be there as early as the 21st, which seemed utterly impossible to me.

My first two weeks I had covered 1,066 miles over the ground, probably sailing fifteen or twenty per cent more than that because of headwinds. Poor progress. I missed the electricity, especially the instruments, and it annoyed me that when it got dark I simply had to go to bed. I tried reading with a flashlight, but it was very uncomfortable. I was in my sleeping bag by ten and always it took me at least two hours to get to sleep, not being accustomed to early bedtimes. I listened to Willis Conover's jazz programme on the Voice of America, and to the American Forces Radio and Television Service, in addition to the BBC. We were too far out for Radio Two now, but I was picking up the American station in the Azores again, and getting the first hard news about the coming Democratic Convention in New York. After reading about him for months in the *International Herald Tribune*, I heard Jimmy Carter's voice for the first time. He sounded very familiar, like half the people I'd grown up around in Georgia.

I became very subject to reminiscence, something that had happened to me on the return trip from the Azores, too. I found myself easily moved by memories and by things I read or heard on the radio which brought back memories. The Northern Service of the Canadian Broadcasting Company was replaying a series of old radio programmes, Inner Sanctum, the Green Hornet and, best of all, Jack Benny. The CBC and VOA also played a lot of music from other eras, and one evening I suddenly found myself in tears, listening to Bob Hope and Marilyn Maxwell, I think, singing 'Baby It's Cold Outside'. It's not a very sentimental song, but I suddenly remembered that when I was about six years old I had known all the lyrics to the male part of that song, and a little girl across the street had known the girl's part. I remembered sitting under a tree in my grandparents' front yard on a hot summer day, singing that duet, while we waited for the local fire department to come and rescue a cat which had been chased up the tree we were sitting under by a local dog. What moved me was the memory that I had had a childhood in which firemen came to rescue cats from trees.

On Sunday, June 20th, I scored what for me was a navigational triumph. I took my first moon sight, plotted it across a sunsight and had an instant position, without having to wait for a noon sight. It doesn't sound like much of an event, but after a while alone at sea, small successes become wildly elating, just as small problems become hugely depressing. While I was doing the plotting I looked up from the chart table and saw through the windows on the port side the bows of a huge ship. I ran up on deck, waving and pointing at the signal flags I kept flying which meant 'Report me to Lloyds'. People on deck waved back and, as I watched, the ship made a ninety degree course change to port and sailed away. Apparently, she had come up on my starboard side, gone astern of me and then run on a parallel course on my port side to see if there was anybody aboard. I had been too absorbed in plotting my position to hear her engines, close as we were. I wondered what the outcome would have been if the encounter had occurred at night.

The calms and light winds persisted, but very gradually the sea became flatter, until it was not unpleasant to be sailing slowly. My log for Monday, June 21st read, in part: *Sitting in the watch seat writing this – a lovely evening. I'm wearing only tennis shorts, and the air feels good on my skin. There is what looks like squally showers up to windward; if it will*

Harp drifts through light airs in mid-Atlantic. The very light drifter genoa kept her moving.

bring a good sailing breeze that's O.K. with me. I have been sitting on the 'back porch' – the self-steering platform – trailing my feet in the cool water. It is very blue and extraordinarily clear. A fish about eighteen inches long appears to have fallen in love with the rudder – he has been swimming alongside, almost touching it, for hours. We were almost completely becalmed from nine a.m. to four p.m. . . . . Spotted a mooring buoy ahead and after what seemed like a very long time, crept abeam of it. It had the number nine on top and the name (I think) Nancy Egary. The owner can find his mooring at 40°27′N, 27°22′W. Heard on BBC that Tabarly is within a day's sail of Newport. If it's true he will beat the record by three days. Seems impossible. . . . The Azores are being even more elusive than on the trip with Bill. Graciosa is still sixty miles away and Flores is a hundred miles further than that. . . .

I was wearing tennis shorts and not running around naked because I had been doing just that, and parts of me which were unaccustomed to the hot sun were complaining. I could sit comfortably only in certain unusual positions. The Azores were, indeed, taking their time about turning up. On the race the year before, Bill and I had taken $15\frac{1}{2}$ days and we had considered that two or three days too long. That night, however, I picked up the loom of a light on Faial and as I was about to go below to plot the bearing, I looked astern and saw two enormous red lights from a position where there could be no land. It was obviously not a ship, and just when I was beginning to reassess my opinions about UFOs, I realized that it was the moon rising, only a sliver of it, but huge and red and broken up by black clouds stretching across it. It was a few minutes before my pulse returned to normal.

Next morning, I could see things growing in my drinking water. This was alarming. I remembered an account by a competitor in the last Race describing a similar experience with his water; he had had to put into the Azores to clean his tanks and change the water. If I wanted an excuse to visit Faial again, here it was. I decided to wait another day before making a decision about it. When I checked it again, I found that the contamination was only in the starboard tank and not the port, and I remembered that Yves Anrys had given me two water purification tablets before the start of the Race. I had put them on the chart table and forgotten what they were. Now they were wedged under the barometer and crumbling, but I swept up the pieces, divided them equally between the two tanks and poured a pint of water in after each of them to make sure they did not lodge in the filler pipes. I reasoned that the contamination was probably harmless bacteria, and anyway, the pills were at work now, so I would drink the starboard tank first, before anything new started growing in it.

My first flying fish. Not exactly a Trade Winds breakfast.

A day later, the water situation was still on my mind when I rose to find Faial, green and lovely, off my port bow, with a cloud-enshrouded Pico behind. The height of the islands, Faial at 3,500 feet and Pico at 7,000 feet, must make them among the best landfalls in the world, when they are not obscured by cloud. I thought of Horta and the people and places I knew there – Augie and Luis, the Club Naval, Peter and his Café Sport, the Estelagem and the village market – and I resolved to come back when I could combine the excitement of seeing the Azores with the satisfaction of visiting them.

The BBC was now reporting that the Race winner was five hundred miles from Newport, but they had stopped mentioning Tabarly specifically. I wondered how Mike McMullen was doing, hoped he was up front, unnoticed and winning. I had thought about Lizzie and Mike often, and I wanted him to be not just the first multihull, but the first boat across the line. I knew that no one else could be as highly motivated.

The water was choppy in the archipelago waters. Faial remained in view for nearly a day-and-a-half in the clear weather, and as I was coming on deck for my noon sight on the 24th, glancing to see if the island was still there, I saw instead a ship coming up fast astern of us. She was *Olwen*, Royal Navy I think, since her officers were in whites, but there were women aboard, too, and I wondered how the Royal Navy had managed that. She passed me, then circled and came close abeam my starboard side, and I shouted through my Tannoy loud-hailer, 'Please report me to Lloyds'.

'I have already done so,' replied an officer from the bridge.

I asked for my position, but he was unable to get the information before his part of the ship passed me, and suddenly *Harp* was *very* close to her, close enough for a rating further aft to ask after my welfare only barely raising his voice. I dropped everything and threw in a very fast tack, and the big ship slid by only a few yards away. That rattled me a bit, and it must have got to her captain, too, for this time he did not circle, but hove to and waited for me to come to him. I was not about to go anywhere near the ship, stopped or not, without an engine. He waited for a few minutes, probably trying to get me on the VHF, because an antenna was visible at my masthead, then sailed on. At least my position would be reported, I thought.

That night I heard on the BBC that Clare Francis was a thousand miles from Newport, apparently on the great circle route. I got out the dividers and measured my distance from the finish. I had made my first turn on my course at about 37°30′N, 35°W, and I still had just over two thousand miles to go. Maybe they were having heavy weather up there, but at least they were having wind, too, while I sat becalmed or in light headwinds day after day. But now I was at my southerly turning point, the place where the reaching winds were supposed to be. If they came, and if they were fresh, my daily runs would improve dramatically. And anyway, didn't they have calms on the great circle route? Maybe there was a chance of making a good showing, yet.

25 Going West

I don't suppose I had really expected fresh reaching winds to materialize the moment I reached a point on the chart, but I was bloody disappointed when they didn't. Still, at the end of three weeks I had covered 1,645 miles over the ground, and my daily average was improving steadily.

Life went on in a regular sort of way, my daily routine continuing. I saw my first sea turtle; he measured about three feet across his shell and was covered in barnacles. We sailed slowly past him in light winds, so slowly that I was able to go below, get a camera and take a couple of shots of him.

Then my eggs went bad. An egg company had given us thirty each, and Yves Anrys had given me his, but for some reason my taste for them had disappeared and I had eaten only two since Plymouth. I had a good time with them now, though. I sat in the cockpit and dropped them overboard one by one, watching as they sank, but remaining in sight for an amazingly long time in the clear water.

I had passed my halfway point and had begun to get out my large-scale charts of the east coast of the United States and mark them up for future use.

On July 28th the BBC reported that the French Navy had started a search for Eric Tabarly. This seemed ridiculous to me, since he had only been out for twenty-two days, and there were any number of good reasons why he might not have appeared in Newport yet. What seemed more a cause for concern was that sixty-seven of the yachts in the Race had not been sighted or heard from either during the past week or since the start. I was glad I was not one of them. It suddenly occurred to me that although I had been seen and my family and friends had news of me, I had none of them and would have none until reaching Newport.

Anything might have happened – someone might be dead or ill – and I would have no way of knowing. It was a facet of singlehanding that had never crossed my mind and I found it mildly discomforting. Colas was reported two hundred miles from Newport after putting into St Johns, Newfoundland, for repairs. This was perfectly proper, since the rules stipulated that a yacht could stop anywhere for as long as her skipper wished, as long as he was not towed for more than two miles into and out of port and observed all the other rules.

The following day, the 29th, I heard that Tabarly had won, crossing the line at nine in the morning, Newport time. Colas was thought to be close behind. I was sorry that Mike McMullen hadn't won, or Mike Kane, but there was still the multihull prize, which I had begun to think of as the 'Tin Lizzie'. Then, the next day, came the amazing news that Michael Birch, in one of the little Newick trimarans, *The Third Turtle*, had finished third, followed closely by Kazimierz Jaworski in his thirty-eight-foot monohull, *Spaniel*. They were both remarkable performances, *Spaniel*'s being perhaps the most remarkable, since she was a monohull. David Palmer, who had expected to win the *Jester* class in *FT*, had dismissed the Newick trio as contenders, saying that a boat completed this season could not win for lack of time to prepare. It was a classic case of a competitor believing that everyone else would experience the same teething problems he had; of not recognizing that there will always be someone, in a race of this size, whose boat is better designed, better prepared and better sailed than yours. Considering all the variables, it was not a race to be cocky about. Here, we had the boat that everyone had predicted would win in a walk coming second, beaten by a boat designed to be sailed by fifteen men, then two yachts from the smallest class finishing third and fourth, ahead of much larger, faster boats which should have beaten them. It was that kind of race.

From my log of July 1st: *I have just dined on sweet and sour ham, with peanuts and raisins, and the 'Batard Montrachet' '70 and am a little bit drunk; Willis Conover is playing very good jazz on the Voice of America and Mike Flanagan is dead. BBC said at midday, as I was eating a ham sandwich, that 'Galloping Gael' has been found by a merchant ship, drifting, with no one aboard. Mike is apparently the victim of what I have always thought is the single most dangerous risk of this Race – falling overboard and watching your boat sail away. It is said that drowning is a pleasant death, but it cannot be pleasant to tread water and contemplate it until it happens. When I heard about this my first action was to put down my sandwich, go and sit on the back porch (first clipping my harness to the pulpit) and rig a tripping line to the self-steering. It is now being towed behind with a number of knots and two loops tied into it. It may not be much, but it is all I can do. I didn't know Mike Flanagan well, but he seemed a nice enough fellow and was, I am told, supremely confident of his chances of winning the 'Jester Trophy'. Now, barring a true miracle, he is gone, a victim of what? The Race? His own self-confidence (vanity)? Or an unavoidable accident? (There are unavoidable accidents.) Now, in the last month, two attractive young people I knew are dead. Why do I feel responsible, or at least guilty? They are not dead because they both knew me, although I may have been their only connection. I have believed from the beginning that someone would die in this Race. Now, someone has. God, let that be an end to it.*

On July 2nd I heard that Colas had been docked ten per cent of his elapsed time for having someone help him hoist his sails in St John's. *(Later information: A member of the Race Committee had telephoned the St John's coast guard to learn the circumstances of Colas' arrival and departure and had been told that on leaving, Colas had taken a party on board with him out of the harbour, thus breaking the most important rule of all, the one about sailing alone. Whether or not he had help with his sails made no difference, and he was lucky to get away with a ten per cent penalty.)*

My radar reflector chaffed through its shackle and slid down the backstay, thus reducing my visibility on radar. I ploughed through my tinned American snack foods, continuing to gain weight and contemplating the disappearance of my navel.

From my log of July 3rd: *Becalmed most of last night and until 11.00 hours this morning. When the wind returned it was, of course, nearly on the nose. I have been irritable all day. If I don't improve my daily average it will take me another three weeks to reach Newport, and we've been at it for four weeks today. We seem to sail (hard on the wind) from one calm to another, like traffic roundabouts on the route, each jammed, with movement non-existent. BBC says that David Palmer and Walter Green finished seventh and eighth (but who was fifth and sixth?). They were both very good performances, finishing ahead of a lot of the 'Pen Duick' and 'Gypsy Moth' classes. Good for them. I hope Mike McMullen was fifth or sixth. Why don't they give us more news? The BBC hasn't had one interview with anybody connected with the Race. Today I am (temporarily) weary of this enterprise, but now that the boat is moving again, in whatever direction, I feel better.*

What I did not write in my log, for fear of giving the idea more credence in my own mind, was the thought that if Mike McMullen were not number five or six, he would not be in Newport when I arrived. I tried to think of all the hundreds of reasons why he might not be among the leaders – broken mast, leaky boat, illness – and still be safe, but the thought would not go away.

As July 4th, 1976, the bicentennial anniversary of the founding of my country dawned, I was still 1300 miles from Newport. Shattered was my hope of being in Newport for the celebration, and shattered it had been for two or three weeks, but that didn't make it feel any better. Now I was worried about finishing the Race before the fifty-day time limit expired. As we rode out a Force seven on the nose, I listened to reports of celebrations from all over the United States on the Voice of America. The Queen was in Newport, hosting a dinner for the President. Pity I couldn't make it. Somebody, probably Protestant terrorists, had planted some bombs in Dublin. I was sad to think that the mindless war was beginning to be felt in the Republic. The Israelis freed the hostages at Entebbe, in Uganda, and I think that was the high point of my day. I stood up and cheered. I read Conrad's *The Nigger of the Narcisus* and then, in a fever of patriotism, wrote a letter to Jimmy Carter, offering to work in his campaign. It would be some time before I could mail it. Thirteen hundred miles to go. Twelve days, with luck. Twice that, without it.

The next day the wind began to rise and back, putting us on course again, but hard on the wind. It blew hard all that night, and I was routed out of bed early the next morning to reef right down to storm canvas. The squall hadn't allowed any time for dressing, so I did the job naked. By the time I had finished the wind was blowing a steady Force ten, and the scene around me was very strange. Here we were in fifty to fifty-five knots of wind (I was certain about that, comparing it to the blow on the trip back from the Azores the year before), and the sun was shining brightly. It was very warm, and I sat naked in the cockpit for half-an-hour or so, watching the enormous seas and delighting in the sunshine. It was delightfully pleasant until the wind increased to the point where the spray hurt like hell, and I had to get below, my skin red as if from a needle shower.

As the storm continued, I began to worry that it might be a hurricane. The hurricane season runs from June to November, but most of them occur in September or October. I got out my Reed's Nautical Almanac and began to read up on hurricane symptoms. They all fitted. I began to think about gybing, to sail away from the centre of a possible tropical storm, which is the standard procedure, but I decided to wait for an hour or so to see what happened to the barometer. I crawled back into my bunk and tied myself in for the wait. A few minutes later I opened my eyes and looked straight up through the starboard window. I could see the cap shroud waving in the breeze. (The mast receives all its lateral support from two wires on each side of the mast. The cap shroud is the outer, longer one. If it goes on the windward side, the mast goes, too.) I ripped the back cushions off the bunk to get at the bosun's bag and a spare clevis pin, found one, grabbed a harness and got on deck, all, it seemed, in a matter of seconds. It was still blowing very hard, and now I had to brace my feet against the toe rail, hang onto the inner shroud and try to catch the waving length of wire rope. Finally I got it, and with trembling hands, managed to get the clevis pin in place and secured. I was just breathing a huge sigh of relief when one of the spinnaker poles, which had been secured to the windward side of the deck, hit me in the back. It was another couple of minutes before I had wrestled that back into place and resecured it. Back inside the cabin, shaking like a leaf, I reflected on what might have happened had I gybed a few minutes earlier; the loose shroud would have then been on the windward side and the mast would have gone.

Less than an hour later we were becalmed again. I couldn't believe it. Almost no wind and still a huge sea left from the storm. Very uncomfortable. But when the wind finally filled in again, it came from the east, which was nearly impossible according to the pilot chart. Not wanting to set a spinnaker in the confused seas, I boomed out the number two genoa, hoisted the full main and we flew before the wind, clocking up 140 miles during the next twenty-four hours, our best day's run, and 120 miles the following day, before the wind veered and headed us again. It was now July 9th and there were less than a thousand miles to go.

With the boat hard on the wind again in a moderate breeze, I stretched out for an afternoon nap. I was nearly asleep when I heard a buzzing sound. The Zenith was tuned to the Voice of America and I thought the Soviets were jamming it again, as they sometimes did, but the buzzing grew quickly into a roar, much louder than any noise the radio could make. I charged into the cockpit, knowing that sound could only be one thing. As I came through the companionway, a single-engined aeroplane roared past our port side, only about fifty feet above the water. I dived back into the cabin for a camera and got back into the cockpit before he could turn for another pass. He turned and started to come straight in towards the boat as I began taking pictures. For a moment I had the feeling that I was about to be strafed, as in those old World War II movies. He flew past and began to turn again. He was Royal Navy and I figured he must be from an aircraft carrier, because even though he was carrying a large fuel tank under his fuselage, the nearest land was Bermuda, about 450 miles away, and I didn't think such a tiny aircraft would have that sort of range. He came back in again, low, along our port side and I could see the lone pilot. I felt a curious

Found! The search plane from the British aircraft carrier *Ark Royal*.

The search plane was closely followed by a rescue helicopter, very reassuring.

kinship with him, both of us singlehanded in the middle of nowhere. He turned and flew away to the east, and I knew he was from a carrier because there was no land in that direction. Next, I thought, we'll have the carrier along, and I settled down in the cockpit to wait for her to appear.

Fifteen minutes later, there was another, different sort of noise, and I opened my eyes to see a helicopter coming straight at us from the north. It occurred to me that although the first pilot had found me and I had waved, I had given him no indication of whether I needed help, so as the chopper passed I gave him a thumbs-up sign. Two crewmen, sitting in an open doorway aft, waved back, and they were off, back to the east again. I waited for a while longer in the cockpit, but the carrier never appeared. I knew, though, that I had been reported, for the first time in three weeks, and I was wildly elated.

I now found myself low on water. The fouled starboard tank was empty and the port tank was less than half full. There was only one bottle of beer left, too, but plenty of wine and food. I had begun to lose weight, now, the snack foods having run out, and I was in good health and excellent spirits. I expected to be in the Gulf Stream soon, and I began to read up on what Adlard Coles and Erroll Bruce had to say about sailing in that great ocean current. None of it was good. The current normally runs at one-half to one and one-half knots, according to the pilot chart, but what I was reading indicated that in places it could run three to five knots and even reverse its normal southwest to northeast direction. The very warm water temperatures caused very changeable weather conditions, too, and nobody seemed able to predict anything about the Gulf Stream.

On the 11th, as I was cooking, I looked out and saw through the port window what looked like a big squall. There had been dark clouds down there all day, but we had been making good progress under shortened sail. I started on deck to have a better look, but stopped with one foot in the cockpit as a thunderstorm, complete with thunder and lightning, struck us. I have never seen anything like it. Visibility came to an end. The self-steering, about eight feet away, disappeared in a wall of grey water. The sea around the boat turned white, churned into foam by the force of the rain. I pulled my foot back inside the hatch and stood on the ladder and watched. I suppose it lasted for about two minutes, and then I was able to get into the cockpit and reef further. I felt lucky that nothing had broken, and I figured it would all blow over as quickly as it had come. It did, but it came again and then again. I have never experienced anything as sudden and as violent as these thunderstorms which raked across us for $2\frac{1}{2}$ days. On land there are trees and buildings

A Gulf Stream thunderstorm about to come roaring in. Winds exceeded fifty knots during these.

to break the force of such storms, but not at sea. Even more frightening than the sixty-knot gusts of wind was the lightning. For the whole of the $2\frac{1}{2}$ days I had the feeling of living under a huge, electrically lit sign which, because of some wiring fault, was flashing on and off erratically. It was all the more frightening because *Harp*'s mast, thirty-eight feet above the water, was the only tall object in hundreds of square miles, and it was made of aluminium, a wonderful conductor of electricity.

Occasionally there was a lull, when the wind would drop to Force six or seven for a few minutes. During one of these, Fred tacked the boat and put us aback. He had done this several times, when the combination of a gust and a wave would push the boat up into the wind a bit, and I was extremely annoyed with him. I had always talked to him, as if he were a dog or cat, and now I found myself screaming at him as I struggled to get the boat back on the right tack in the big seas, 'You sonofabitch! You do that again and I . . . I won't oil you any more!'

About seven-thirty in the evening of the 13th the wind had dropped enough to unreef, and for the first time in what seemed like years, the horizon to windward was not filled with dark thunderheads. I released the reefing line to the Dynafurl and started to crank in on the sheet to shake out the reefing genoa, pleased because we were only about four hundred miles out of Newport now, and I was hoping to cross the line on Friday, the 16th. That would give me a reasonably creditable passage of forty days – more than I had wanted to take, but not bad. Something

The Irish Tri-Colour all-rounder—the only time I was able to set a spinnaker.

stuck. The sail would not come unreefed. Swearing under my breath, I hauled the sheet in as tight as it would go, made it fast, got into a harness and crawled onto the foredeck, where I began turning the swivelled forestay by hand. Suddenly, the forestay wasn't there any more. There was a metallic thunking noise and the whole stay, sail and all, flew out of my hands, the aluminium reel at the bottom nearly hitting me in the face. I had been squatting, turning the stay, and now I was dumped back onto my bum, watching the forestay, which supported the mast from forward, waving the number two genoa in the breeze from the top of the mast like a giant flag. First the stay, now the stick, I thought.

I sat on the foredeck and waited for the mast to go.

26 Drifting in the Gulf Stream

Incredibly, the mast did not break. The wind was down to about Force three, the main was double reefed, and the inner forestay held everything together long enough for me to charge aft and release the main sheet and start getting halyards forward. Fortunately, *Harp* was equipped with two genoa halyards and two spinnaker halyards, and I got three of this lot forward to the toe rail and winched them tight. The mast would not fall now, but there was the immediate problem of recovering the flailing forestay and sail before the fitting at the top of the mast broke under the strain and sent everything overboard.

After twenty minutes of fruitless effort, trying to haul everything down onto the deck by hand, I discovered the easy way: I put the windward sheet onto one of the big Barlow self-tailing winches and cranked away until the stay was back on deck and under control. Perhaps 'under control' is an overstatement, for the aluminium rod forestay was writhing all over the place like a giant serpent. Finally, I got it shackled to the toe rail and lashed it so that it could not thrash about and chafe things. Next, I got the sail off, with some difficulty, and stowed. This gave me another genoa halyard to play with, and now the wisdom of having the little storm jib made came home to me. I set this flying on the halyard, tacked to the pad eye which had been fitted about two feet abaft the forestay tack, and once again we had a headsail and could go to windward. We couldn't point very high, but we could go to windward, and that's where Newport was.

Trouble was, now that the wind had dropped and we had been reduced to a double-reefed main and a storm jib, we could only move at about two knots. I was afraid to hoist the whole main for fear of putting too much strain on the halyards and toe rail forward. Making two knots there was no chance of reaching Newport by the weekend, and this was very depressing. Still, things could have been a great deal worse; we could have lost the mast and really have been in trouble. Our reduced speed called for a reassessment of the food and water situation, too. Food was getting short and water even shorter, so I had to be very careful to see that nothing else happened to delay us, or I would have to go on a very serious diet. I had already started brushing my teeth in salt water, and now I watched every drop. I tried collecting more water in the thunder-showers by hanging a bucket from the end of the boom; this worked for a while, then the bucket <u>blew away</u>. But at least we had a main and a headsail and, above all, a mast.

unsecured!

Twenty-four hours later, however, we didn't have a headsail any more. The halyard on which it was flying parted at the mast sheave, probably because, in an effort to get the luff of the sail tight, I had winched it up too much and it was carrying too much of the weight of the mast. I was afraid to set the sail on another halyard – I was running out of them – and we made little progress during the night under the reefed main only.

I decided to have a go at getting my VHF transmitter working with spare batteries from my signalling lamp. They were six volts each; six plus six equalled twelve, I reasoned, and the VHF worked on a twelve-volt current. I wired the two batteries together, hooked them to the radio and it worked! At least, I was getting crackling noises. I didn't want to try transmitting until I could see a ship, since the batteries were small and surely wouldn't last long.

By morning it was clear that under the present sail plan we could sail either to Newfoundland or Bermuda, but not to Newport, unless we got a radical wind shift, and I wasn't going to count on that. The only alternative seemed to be to repair the forestay in some way so that we could set a headsail, a job which seemed clearly impossible. It was bad enough that when the stay was unshackled from the toe rail it would start thrashing about again; but the main problem would be getting the stay to stretch enough to reach the forestay tack. I had found the cause of the failure; a deck eye which fitted into the bottom of the forestay had come unscrewed. First, I removed the deck eye from the forestay tack and tried to screw it back into the bottom of the stay. The threads were stripped. It would go part of the way in, then freewheel when turned. I spent two hours, lying on my side on the foredeck, draped over a spinnaker pole, trying to get the thing screwed back in. Finally, using a large screwdriver for leverage, I managed by putting pressure on it and turning at the same time, to get it most of the way in. But I had no way of knowing if the threads would hold and keep the same thing from happening again.

Now I had to try to stretch the forestay far enough to reach its deck fitting. The logical thing to do, of course, was to ease off the backstay, then crank down on the halyards forward, bending the mast until it reached. But I knew that would not get it close enough. O.H. and I, when *Harp* had been relaunched at the beginning of the season, had had one hell of a time getting the backstay to reach under similar circumstances, and that was with two of us pulling on it and no sea tossing us about. I would have to find another way.

My eye fell on the reefing line, which had broken when the stay went. This was a length of flexible wire rope with a rope tail spliced to one end for ease of handling. I took the block normally used for the spinnaker foreguy and shackled it to the forestay tack fitting, then ran the reefing line up through it and tied it around the wire drum at the bottom of the forestay. I took the rope tail back to a winch and cranked it as tight as I could, then went back to inspect the angle at which the line was drawing the forestay towards its fitting. It looked right, but there was still a twelve-inch gap between the end of the stay and the deck fitting. I went back to the cockpit and cranked each halyard down as tight as I could, then cranked on the reefing line again. It was working. I loosened the backstay even more and cranked down on all the winches again. The gap was now only about two inches. Was it possible this was going to work?

I cranked still further and the reefing line parted. It wasn't going to work. I was going to have to sail to Newfoundland and try to keep from starving to death while I was doing it. I ran the line through the block again and retied it, then went back and started easing off the backstay even more, frightened stiff that I would turn the wheel one thread too many and the backstay would go. I eased it about two inches beyond where I thought it would be safe then, one by one, cranked down on the halyards again, then the reefing line. I went forward to inspect the gap. The deck eye was $\frac{1}{4}$ inch from the position where the clevis pin would slip in to secure it. Summoning up all the strength I had, I squeezed the eye into the gap. The clevis pin went in. With trembling hands I secured it with a split pin, and we had a forestay again.

I couldn't believe it. I had done something that two men shouldn't have been able to do in a seaway. Could Robin Knox-Johnston have done this? (Of course he could, and in half the time.) The job had taken me from ten that morning until early evening, and I was too exhausted to hoist a foresail, so we slogged on overnight under main only. The next day was the 16th, the day I had planned to arrive in Newport, and we had drifted thirty-five miles to the northeast, pushed by the Gulf Stream. When the forestay broke we had been about four hundred miles from Newport, on about the latitude of Cape May. Now we were further north, and I was worried about being headed again, as we would not be able to point high to windward with the present state of the rigging.

On the Friday morning I thought I would try to pick up Nantucket Light Ship, as we were getting close to being within radio direction finding range. I couldn't hear Nantucket Light Ship, but I was picking up another signal loud and clear. I checked the chart in Reed's, showing all the New England radio beacons, and none of them matched the morse code I was hearing. I began running through the lists of other east coast beacons, and in a moment my finger froze. I was hearing a radio beacon on the coast of *North Carolina*, and it had an effective range of *a hundred miles.* Had I, through some navigational blunder, approached the coast in the wrong place? Was I really off North Carolina? I began twirling dials furiously, weak with apprehension. I found another beacon and hurriedly looked it up. Cape Cod Light. I nearly fainted. Apparently, some freak atmospheric condition had allowed me to pick up the North Carolina beacon so clearly. For confirmation, I switched on the Zenith and started looking for commercial stations. The thunderstorms had caused so much interference that I had been unable to pick up anything except short-wave for several days. I found a station in Lynn, Massachusetts. I felt better.

[handwritten marginal note: no: Home to Georgia!]

Now my biggest concern was being becalmed. After the violence of the thunderstorms, we were down to about a Force two and it was coming from, of all places, the east. I got up a spinnaker, hoisting the heavier all-rounder, because if the wind rose I didn't want to do another spinnaker change. We ran for most of the day in a light breeze then, about sunset, the wind began to rise and go around. Soon we were close reaching at about seven knots and I was steering, because Fred couldn't handle the helm under those conditions. I took the spinnaker down at dark and got up the number two genoa, hoping that the dodgy forestay fitting and the two halyards still taken forward to the toe rail would keep the mast up. We managed an eighty-mile run that day, and I was pleased and relieved. That night, after dark, I thought I could detect a change of colour in the water. The edge of the Gulf Stream is easier to find in the north than in the south. The water temperature and the colour change very quickly at the edge. Next morning, the colour was a dirty brown instead of the deep blue to which I had become accustomed.

We had the mast, we had a foresail and we were out of the Gulf Stream. Newport lay ahead. We were finally in the home stretch.

A ship's horn at this range is a sure-fire alarm-clock.

Gazing into my last sunset at sea. The moustache, so carefully cultivated, went soon after my arrival in Newport. It made me look less like Clarke Gable than I had planned.

27 The final dash

Sunday morning, the 18th, I picked up a Newport commercial radio station. I could not have been more excited if I had been contacted by a flying saucer. I could hear people talking, and they were in Newport, Rhode Island. What's more, they were reporting Race news. Five or six boats had finished during the last twenty-four hours, including Ziggy Puchalski and Richard Konklowski; another twenty-five boats still had not finished, so at least I wouldn't be last.

I had a good lunch and stretched out on a settee berth for a nap. A few minutes later, as I was sleeping soundly, I was lifted right off the berth by the sound of a ship's foghorn at what seemed a distance of about eighteen inches. I landed in the cockpit, ready to dive overboard and swim for it. There, about fifty yards off the port quarter, was a large merchant ship, *Alchemist*. I jumped below to get the loudhailer, not wanting to use the tiny radio batteries unless absolutely necessary. I started to shout that I wanted to send a telegram, but she was already overtaking us. Someone on the bridge made a hand signal to indicate that they would circle. I tried to wave them off, remembering my close call with *Olwen* some weeks before, but they circled and came up again. I shouted out a telegram to Angela in Newport, giving an ETA of Tuesday and asked for a position. But we were being overtaken again, and the big ship circled a second time. This time, the radio operator was standing on the foredeck, and as I shouted out my message, he sprinted towards the stern of his ship, writing furiously. Someone on the bridge had an old-fashioned hand megaphone and shouted a position to me. It struck me as funny that I, on my tiny boat should have an excellent loudhailer, while they, on their huge ship, should have a megaphone.

They sailed on, promising to dispatch my telegram immediately. My spirits soared now. My position had been reported, my navigation had proved to be perfect, and in two days I would be in Newport. I anticipated arriving between noon and three with the light winds we were experiencing. Then, only a few minutes after the disappearance of *Alchemist*, I looked off the port quarter and saw a yacht, the first I had seen since the English Channel. She was in the far distance, and even with the binoculars I could not recognize her, but I felt sure she was a competitor. She was there for the rest of the day, slowly overtaking us, and during the night she disappeared.

While I was watching her I saw something else in the water, a float of some kind, with a pole and a radar reflector. Then another, and another. This meant I would have to keep a lookout for fishing boats that night and the next, but also that they were using radar to find their floats, so would be likely to spot me, even though my reflector had slipped down to about six feet above the deck.

Darkness fell and I kept a close watch, sometimes lying down for ten minutes at a time to rest, but not falling asleep. About two-thirty in the morning, as I was resting, I was suddenly overcome by a violent chill. Shaking uncontrollably, I got up to light the cabin heater, but thought I would first have a look around. I stuck my head up through the hatch to find a large fishing boat two hundred yards dead ahead, bearing down on us at about ten knots. I grabbed a torch and signalled him, and he changed course to pass about twenty-five yards on our starboard side. The chill vanished. Had I developed another level of perception, like Bill King? Maybe.

Monday, July 19th, our last day out. The wind backed and freshened and we were tearing along at six knots under our reefing genoa and double-reefed main. My ETA began to change, and for once, to earlier. We saw no shipping of any sort that day until sunset, when the first fishing boat appeared. At midnight, a huge, brightly lit ship, looking like an aircraft carrier, appeared on the horizon and tore across our wake several miles astern at very high speed.

We had now picked up Gay Head Light on Martha's Vineyard to starboard, and Buzzard's Bay Light was ahead, off the starboard bow. I kept a running check on our position with bearings from the two lights, combined with a check of our depth. At midnight I estimated we were fifteen miles from Brenton Reef Light and the finishing line, but I would not yet see it, even though it should have been visible at that distance. I hoped that one of the infamous local fogs was not enshrouding Newport – that was all I needed. I was taking great care to see that nothing went wrong this close to the finish. I kept thinking about Bill Howell in the last Race, about to finish in fifth place, then colliding with a fishing boat. I didn't want that sort of problem now. My

ETA was now three a.m. I had not wanted to arrive at night in a strange port and I hoped I would be met at the finishing line, as had been mentioned at the pre-race briefing.

At twenty minutes past midnight I saw Brenton Reef Light, flashing in the distance. I abandoned my compass course and began steering for the light, the first time in forty-five days I had had a mark to steer for. It was very satisfying. At 01.45, Judith Point Light appeared, and from bearings on the two lights I estimated my distance at seven miles. An hour later, I was almost on top of Brenton Reef Light and looking hard for the flashing red light on the buoy that marked the other end of the finishing line. I could see the lights of Newport arrayed behind the light.

I brought some flares, the signalling torch and the loudhailer into the cockpit. I didn't want to waste a minute being found when I was across. The red buoy appeared where it was supposed to be.

On July 20th, 1976, at 03.15 local time, 07.15 GMT, *Golden Harp* crossed the finishing line. The second we cleared the line I stood up on the afterdeck and struck a white flare. The yacht lit up as if a dozen Klieg lights had been thrown on it. I had never seen such an intense, white light. The flare burned for about a minute, then sputtered out, leaving me with no night vision whatever. Gradually, my eyes became accustomed to the darkness again, and there was no boat of any kind to be seen. The wind was dropping very quickly, and *Harp* was slowing, now running dead before it at about two knots. I waited a few minutes and struck another flare. Again, the intense light, followed by equally intense darkness. Still no other boat.

Following the chart as best I could, we started up the river towards Newport. The lights of the town and of the large suspension bridge further up the river made it very difficult to pick out buoys and lights ashore. The wind continued to drop and soon we were barely stemming the tide. We drew abeam of where Castle Hill coast guard station was marked on the chart. I could see a large building on a hill, with several exterior lights. I signalled the station, but there seemed to be no one on watch. (The building was a hotel. The coast guard station was behind the hill.) I tried the VHF, but got no reply either from the coast guard or from Goat Island Marina, where a twenty-four hour watch was being kept at a reception centre being run by American Tobacco. Nothing. Maybe the small batteries were enough for receiving, but not for transmitting. I struck another flare abeam of the coast guard station. Still no notice was taken of me.

I sat in the river for the rest of the night, fuming at being ignored. Forty-five days at sea and no bands, no fireworks, no dancing girls, not even a rowboat. The river was absolutely devoid of traffic of any kind.

These people did not seem to understand my heroic achievement. Did they think I did this every day? Shit.

Dawn came as slowly as possible. I made a cup of coffee and tried to stay awake until somebody else was up. I wondered what time the local water skiers got started; there didn't seem to be anybody else stirring. There was still not enough wind to make any headway against the tide.

At six o'clock I heard an engine. Reception committee? Fishing boat. He was on his way out for his day's work, passing a hundred yards to starboard. I hailed him and asked if he would call Goat Island Marina on his radio and ask them to come and get me. He said he would, and I settled down with my coffee again. A couple of minutes later, he had turned and was coming alongside.

'Nobody's up,' he said. 'Throw me a line, I'll take you in.' The only other person aboard his boat was a girl.

'I envy you your crew,' I said. 'I haven't seen one of those for six weeks.' She laughed and made my line fast.

As we moved up the river a huge, red sun rose behind the spires of Newport. I stood on the deck and looked at the houses and green shore. It seemed unreal, a New England Disneyland, constructed of *papier mâché*. We approached the Marina's fuel dock. A lone figure stood on the pier, holding a towel. I shouted at him to take a line. He did. He was waiting for someone to come and unlock the showers. I called the reception centre. No answer; it had closed the day before. Customs wasn't up yet. No need to wake Angela at this hour. I lurched back to the yacht on my new land legs and pottered around the decks, sorting ropes, then went below for another cup of coffee. I was too excited to sleep. A voice from above. I stuck my head up. A smiling face greeted me.

'I'm Pete Dunning; I run the Marina; I think you're the sixty-third boat in. Congratulations.'

'Where's Mike McMullen?'

'He hasn't been reported since the start of the Race.'

I knew it. I think I had known it all along.

Epilogue

I had my first hot shower in six weeks, and Angela turned up soon afterwards, having been rung by Pete Dunning. I got all the news: 125 boats had started the Race; I had finished sixty-third; thirty-six had retired in various stages of damage; five had sunk, but their skippers were rescued; Mike Flanagan was lost and Mike McMullen was missing. Several other boats had not been reported, but were eventually accounted for.

There was much discussion about what had happened to Mike McMullen. It was the consensus among those who knew him that he would not have taken his own life, even after having lost Lizzie. He seemed too good a yachtsman and too familiar with his boat and her limitations to have lost her in heavy weather. No collision had been reported. It is my own view that he went in some simple, everyday way, probably falling overboard like Mike Flanagan and like Brian Cooke the year before. That can happen to anybody, no matter how good he is. It is unlikely that anyone will ever know for sure, of course. The only possible consolation for any of his friends is that, depending on the way things really are, he might be with Lizzie. Anyone who knew them will spend the rest of his life missing them.

I pottered around Newport for a couple of weeks, getting small repairs done to *Harp*. My Mother had been in Newport when I arrived and said she was getting tired of the family business. I had decided to sell the yacht and spend some time reorganizing things and getting her retired. I had a novel to finish, too, and the day after I arrived in Newport I talked with Ron Holland about a new boat for the next Race, a bigger and faster boat. It was a very satisfying experience to finish the Race, but I want to do it again, and faster.

Newport is a pleasant and hospitable place. Angela and I saw a lot of

At last, a tow into Newport.

Peter Crowther of *Galway Blazer* and his girl, Pauline, and David Cowper of *Airdale* and his wife, Caroline. Jerry Cartwright and his wife, Kay, had a lot of the competitors over for dinner, and other dinner parties took place on the various yachts and at the Black Pearl on Bowen's Wharf.

There was much warm camaraderie among the finishers and each time another yacht finished, there was much shaking of hands and swapping of stories. Most of the early finishers had gone by the time I reached Newport, but many competitors were still there. A lot of them left the day after my arrival to return via a race to Horta, then France. Tom Grossman of *Cap 33*, who had finished fifth, came down on a visit from Boston. The people of Newport invited us to beach parties and made us feel welcome. They had had an active summer, what with the Tall Ships, then us.

Angela came back to Georgia with us for a few days before returning to London and her job on the *Observer*.

The Race rules are being rewritten, probably to exclude giant yachts, and that may be for the best. There has been the usual chorus from some of the yachting press that the Race be abolished or made into a two-man event. No matter what is said, it seems impossible to make them understand what this Race means to the people who compete in it. Many human beings need adventure, real adventure, personal adventure and, sometimes, as in our case, solitary adventure. Some men and women have always needed that, finding their own physical limits without the

Tabarly, now a French national hero.

Clare Francis celebrates her July 4th arrival in Newport.

aid of bearers and Sherpa guides, searching out their own emotional and spiritual boundaries in places where there is no one to answer to but God. As our society grows and our environment shrinks, there will be more and more little men who will wish to deny us that. Many of them have public or editorial platforms and they will use them to attack this event. They must be ignored.

It is interesting to note that at the start of the Race, where chaos had been predicted, not one untoward incident occurred which could be attributed to the size of the Race, its organization or the singlehanded-ness of its entries. During the remainder of the race only two collisions with ships occurred, one of them not serious, one resulting in the sinking of the yacht and the subsequent rescue of her skipper. Another competitor, Nigel Lang in *Galadriel*, had the truly incredible experience of colliding with another singlehanded yacht, not a competitor, hundreds of miles out in the Atlantic. Neither was seriously damaged.

Two lives were lost, the first ever in this event. It was inevitable that it would happen in one of these Races, and now it has. Both men knew that it might, though neither probably expected it would happen to him. Both, in a sense, died defending the right of men to risk dying in adventurous living.

No one has proposed, with any effect, that motor racing be prohibited or that men stop trying to climb Everest. It is simply accepted that those who participate in these enterprises do so at their own risk, and good luck to them. Those of us who race singlehanded ask no more than that. Leave us alone; ignore us, if you like, but let us get on with it.

Let us, as Jack Oddling-Smee, Commodore of the Royal Western Yacht Club, has said, '. . . enjoy and profit by what must surely be one of the last great freedoms granted to us in this ever contracting world.'